Praise for
Woman Plans, God Laughs

"Deborah has managed her MS journey with humor and courage which will resonate with others who have a chronic illness or their life journey has taken an unexpected turn. People can live well even while they are managing a chronic illness!"

— Dr. Beverly Gilder, M.D. Neurology, MS Specialist

"Deborah managed her MS optimistically and was happy and able to participate in clinical studies to treat her MS and to help further the research being done for all people with Multiple Sclerosis."

— Dr. Ronald Murray, Neurologist

"Debie shared her story with our group and was an encouragement to others."

— Deborah Dinneen, MS Patient in MS Support Group

"Debie Monax's book succeeds in sharing the challenges in her life with the purpose of supporting others. Monax connects her heart to that of her reader through sharing her struggles as she gradually finds grace and acceptance of her circumstances. By reflecting on her life's twists and turns, she inspires all of us to view our difficulties by looking for hidden gifts and finding gratitude even when our plans take a different direction than we expected. Well done!"

— Lisa J. Shultz, Author of *A Chance to Say Goodbye: Reflections on Losing a Parent*

Woman Plans, God Laughs

Woman Plans, God Laughs

My Story of Love, Loss and Learning to Live Life with Faith

Debie Monax

Woman Plans, God Laughs: My Story of Love, Loss and Learning to Live Life with Faith

Published by Bonnie Brae Publishing
Littleton, Colorado

Library of Congress Control Number: 2017915173
MONAX, DEBIE, Author
Woman Plans, God Laughs
Debie Monax

ISBN: 978-0-692-90780-1

BIOGRAPHY & AUTOBIOGRAPHY / Women
BIOGRAPHY & AUTOBIOGRAPHY / Personal Memoirs

QUANTITY PURCHASES: Schools, companies, professional groups, clubs, and other organizations may qualify for special terms when ordering quantities of this title. For information, email Books@BonnieBraePublishing.com.

This book is printed in the United States of America.

BONNIEBRAE
PUBLISHING

To my husband Paul and daughter Sierra,
thank you for believing in me and this project;

to David L. and Frank L. DuMond, Frances Alexander, and
Jessie Collins Veirs, my family of writers,
thanks for your stories;

to all members of my DuMond family,
thank you for believing in me;

to my family of future storytellers–Denise, Don,
Barbara, and Sierra–know that the world Awaits;

and to Matthew, who Jesus took to Heaven too soon, and
who is always in my heart.

Contents

INTRODUCTION

What you are about to read is a story that was meant to be written. The facts written here actually happened. It might seem like a macabre comedy. It is a comedy in places. On the other hand, you could consider it a tragedy; parts of it certainly are. Of all the ways you might choose to read this story, please remember that it truly happened. I completed writing most of this story in 2012, but at that time I wasn't ready to move forward with the publishing stages. However, my desire to share the story never left me. The manuscript sat on the shelf almost as if aging in a barrel to prepare for launch. Then, I met Polly Letofsky at My Word Publishing, and I found the team that would help me to share my story. The events I share are part of the tapestry of my life. Because God makes things perfectly and He is intentional about each life on this planet, I wear that filter when I look back on all that has happened so far. I believe that one of the reasons I'm here on this earth is to share my story with others. I've lived through very difficult experiences, which I will tell you about, and yet I've survived and thrived and am living as a happy, vibrant human being. I will offer you some of my solutions and coping mechanisms which helped me cope and live joyfully again. My hope is that my stories will help you move through your personal life experiences more peacefully. One of my strong hopes is that by hearing about my experiences, you will be able to see and understand someone else's experience compassionately and be there for them in a new way.

I am a forty-something woman as I write this. I am married to Paul, my wonderful husband, who you will read more about. As a family, we like to do outdoor activities like hiking and skiing and have a pop-up trailer we use for camping. We live in beautiful Colorado where the choices of outdoor activities are unlimited. We are grateful for all we have and especially our life with each other.

Mainly, this book is about my adult experiences. I have included some childhood memories as background to help explain my worldview. I loved my family and felt lucky to be a part of a family of six. I was the first of four children and was lucky to have my brother Dan, the second child, as my good friend. We were thirteen months apart. We had to wait a little bit of time, but then we lucked out and got my second brother Don as the third child. At that point, I was feeling out-numbered as one of two females in the family when there were three males around. I absolutely could not wait for the arrival of my sister Denise two years after Don. I wished so hard for a sister and was ecstatic when she was born! Having a sister of my own was incredible to me.

My father was in the Air Force, and my mother stayed home and took care of the household. We tended to stick together because we moved from place to place together as a family. We had unique experiences traveling when one of our moves was to England. For the first time in my life I could see how I fit into the world as a World Citizen, not only as an American. I'm deeply patriotic but have a broad worldview. I took two years of British 20th Century History in school in England to balance out my one year of Honors US History class in American high school. I always believed that my childhood was amazing. I've always felt blessed and special to have the background and experiences that I've had.

In school, I always loved to explain and tell people what kind of family I had. My mom was petite with straight brown hair and blue eyes and was right-handed. My father, on the other hand was very tall with wavy brown hair and hazel eyes and was a leftie. The four kids were amazingly balanced phenotypically. Two boys, two girls; two right-handed, two left-handed; two hazel eyes, two blue eyes; two short, two tall; two straight-haired, two curly-haired. When I learned biology in England and we were learning genetics, I only had to look at my parents and then my siblings to fully understand the science! To me, it was the luckiest set up for a kid. I was proud of my family and cared immensely about them. I was very close to my brother Dan, and we were playmates. I got to see Don and Denise grow up from babyhood and babysit and take care of them. My brother Dan and I used to go into my brother Don's room when he was about two to see what he was doing and look at him. When he was starting to talk, he had his own language that would make us laugh. One time we went into his room, and he shouted Dee Dye! Intensely; Dan and I fell to the floor laughing.

I loved my baby sister Denise. It was astonishing to see her grow and develop over the years. I had some mixed experiences taking care of and worrying about her when I was just a kid myself. On one occasion when I was about eight or nine we went out to eat at a restaurant Casa Bonita in Denver. I was paired up with her in the line to carry one tray to the table with both of our meals on it. I struggled to balance the tray, make sure the plates weren't sliding, and to make sure she was staying with me in the crowd as we followed the hostess to our table. I was as surprised as anybody when I heard the sound before I felt our food sliding off the tray onto the floor. It was an impressive if not embarrassing hullabaloo as clattering sounds of drinks, food, and silverware echoed across the floor before making a huge mess. I was humiliated, and I'm sure Denise was shaken up and scared too!

Over the years and during all the moves we made for my Dad's work, which I will tell you about, I felt close to and felt empathy with each sibling at every stage and wherever we were. Even though we had unique experiences because we were in different grades in school, we still had the shared experiences of going to a new school in a new way, meeting new teachers, adjusting to the different culture and environment at our new schools. In England, Dan and I walked a block and a half and took the city bus by paying 38 pence each way to Rossett High School. Don and Denise walked through the neighborhood from our house to the Pannal Primary School. A quirk in an English school compared to an American one is when they called roll call and said your name, you were to respond with either Miss or Sir depending on whether you had a female or male teacher. The English students had an English accent. So, phonetically, if you had a male teacher and the teacher called names, it would sound like, "William... Sih (classy British voice), Thomas...Sih (classy British voice), Debie...Serr (awkward American sounding voice)." Over the time at school, I would sometimes attempt an authentic English Sih, but I could never quite pull it off without feeling phony. It could be emotionally difficult to move for each of us and at various ages, but we enjoyed a special family bond. I always felt a tremendous loyalty to each person in my family. I liked being part of what to me was a large family. I felt lucky to take long car trips and travel to national parks and other vacations that we did. I knew many kids that I felt, didn't have it as great as I did.

Chapter 1

GROWING UP

What we think we become,
All that we are arises with our thoughts,
With our thoughts, we make the world.
— Buddha

My father was an officer in the Air Force, a fact that I always admired. I knew and felt how very proud he was of his accomplishments. I didn't always know or understand what he did, but I knew it was important. He was larger than life in my family, and I respected him tremendously growing up. So, I was a kid who wanted to be smart like my Dad and earn his respect too. Combine this with my propensity to be an overachiever, and I had a perfect set-up to build myself up as a perfectionist. It was like a seed planted inside a greenhouse. Over the years, with careful attending and watering, I was growing and growing and becoming an exceptional perfectionist! From a very young age, I had figured out and learned that it was important to be good in school, I should always do things that would make my Dad proud, and he would feel that I was successful. By first grade, my teacher Mrs. Wooten spoke to me privately and to my Mom about how I didn't have to work so hard to be perfect. I was learning to write, and I had a persistent goal to write my sentence practice better than anyone else. You see, if you were great, your work would be put up on the bulletin board. I completed those assignments with the vision and plan that I would try to be up on the board each week. Imagine my devastation when, of course, I wasn't on the board each week, and there were always others doing great work too!

Anyone with any experience with the military should have had their ears perk up at reading about my Dad's military career. I was a classic 'military brat' in the sense that my father got transferred because of his job. I was born in California and went to some preschool; then we moved to Omaha, Nebraska when I was four. I spent preschool and half of kindergarten in Omaha, and we moved for a short six months to Virginia where I spent the second half of kindergarten. Then we moved for what I thought could be the last time to Colorado. I kept believing this could be true and I kept a countdown after one year, two years, three years, four years; a sigh of relief, and then halfway through fifth grade, we were moved to California again. This move was devastating to me, but I still had tremendous loyalty to my father and my family. Of course, I would go and make the best of it, but even now I wonder what I might have been if I could have stayed in any one place. I was an active and involved kid, and each move left a trail of dropped hobbies and activities. In

Colorado, I danced ballet and tap and auditioned and performed in the Nutcracker. I learned to play the flute, and I learned to swim and dive.

In California, I adjusted and made new friends. I dropped ballet and tap dancing, but I kept playing the flute; I was the first chair and even became the band's Drum Major to lead the school marching band in parades. I danced in our school talent show two different years to dances my friends and I choreographed. In middle school, I tried out and made it onto a performance dance team, which was jazz dancing. I *loved* it! I gave up diving but still loved swimming. I had one of my first and most heart crushing 'failures' (you know, where I wasn't perfect! Gasp!). I tried out to be a cheerleader and ... didn't get selected! I had zero skills to help me deal with that loss. I thought that if I found out how to do it, did the right things; I would always get the outcome I expected.

I felt somewhat responsible for the next move because my Dad called me in to talk about the possible move to find out what I thought. I was fourteen at the time, so clearly, I wasn't responsible, but later, I carried the burden of the resulting situations. The potential move was to England. I told my Dad how great I thought that would be. In my imagination, foreign countries were hardly believable places to me. It's hard to see how I could have felt that way when now the economy is global, and communication is instant with Facebook and Twitter. I had wild visions of castles and downtown London, and I thought my Dad would be nuts not to take advantage of the opportunity.

This time, we knew pretty much up front that this would be a two-year assignment, three at the outside. Again, I started the horrible, often repeated process of saying goodbye to my best friends, planning to write letters and seeing each other again when I came back home. The planning and implementation of the move was complicated for my parents, but I was familiar with the part in which I got involved. My Mom usually had us kids 'babysit' the movers. Several men would come to our house to pack all our belongings. Typically, one man per bedroom could handle all the tasks. I would sit casually and watch the man in my room. I tried to act like I did this all the time, but I tried not to stare, because I was trying to be polite. The man rarely made conversation. The monotonous routine began:

The mover built a cardboard moving box for knick knacks and dishes, then he would wrap each item in paper;

The mover put items in the box until full and did the tasks below;

Close cardboard box with tape;

Put a sticker on the box for inventory.

I tell you the details because I remember being very uncomfortable and sad to move. I watched the movers who were adults and felt uncomfortable when I was just sitting there watching while they worked. However, I felt the burden of responsibility to make sure everything went right in the moving process, and that was stressful. We never had any problems other than occasionally items got broken in the move. I think my Mom thought a mover we watched and could hold accountable was an honest mover.

Our move was more complicated this time than usual since it was an overseas move. Most of our belongings would be boxed, and put on a pallet and later loaded onto a ship. That meant that we wouldn't see them for eight weeks, which seemed like a lifetime. My Dad had found our new house in Harrogate, England where we would be living. Because we already knew we were moving into a much smaller house, my parents made the decision to put most of our furniture into storage. Thus, boxed items and furniture were to go on the boat, boxed items and furniture for storage, and since it would be so long to get our things, we also had to choose what to pack in our suitcases. In most instances, we took clothes and maybe some toys with us. Adding to the complexity, we needed clothes for summertime in the US, because we were going to drive cross-country to see family, then sell our car before flying to London. Then, we needed to take along England weather clothes to wear until our belongings arrived.

Although I felt an unnecessary burden personally, I can now really appreciate and commend my parents since they were the adults in this process. Our move was successful in the end with one broken item. The cross-country drive to visit relatives was great since we always enjoyed seeing them. We visited my Aunt Pam and her family and were lucky to time it right, arriving twelve days after the birth of my cousin Katrina Jeanne. I felt so blessed by that and remember holding her by myself and feeling like I was holding a valuable gem. I have a wonderful memory of her birth, which I treasure. I didn't know we would lose her in a tragic accident when she was eight years old. Now, this melancholy memory is woven into the fabric of my life and perspective. I will never forget her and am lucky and grateful to my mom and aunt for getting us together frequently so that I have many vivid memories of her.

We went to Macon, Georgia to visit my Aunt Gladys and Uncle Bob. We had a Shetland dog that we got as a puppy named Bonnie Brae. The government rules in England were not conducive to bringing a dog into the country. She would have had to be put into quarantine in a shelter for a long enough time that we thought it would be hard on her. Luckily, my Aunt Gladys and Uncle Bob not only took her to care for her, but they were willing to watch her just for the two years until we came back. What I remember most about that visit was saying goodbye to my aunt and uncle, my Dad driving us all in the station wagon as usual, and looking out the back window of the car and seeing our precious dog Bonnie watching us leave. She had the expectation that we would be right back, but we were not coming back. That was another sad moment in a trail of sad moments involved in that move from California to England. I sat and cried (we all did) as we drove away.

We drove to Michigan to see our aunts, uncles, and cousins there. After another tearful goodbye, we drove to Washington D.C. where my Dad finished some business, and we sold our car. Even getting rid of that car was hard. It was a classic '70s wood-sided station wagon. We called it 'the yellow banana' after my parents had it painted yellow at Earl Scheib because the wood siding was cracked. The paint job did not end up looking much better than it had before! My brother Dan and I had been toddlers when we bought the car, and we still remembered sitting in the back, pop-up seats without car seats or seat belts (unheard of now, but pretty normal in the '70s) when my Dad backed into a tree on a camping trip. Dan and I were sitting across from each other and laughing. When the car hit the tree, we mirrored each other gruesomely in slow motion as the car stopped sharply, and our little heads hit the back door of the station wagon *hard*. Our laughter turned to tears, my brother and I have an indelible memory of the experience, and our new car had a ding in the back the entire time we owned it.

We did some sightseeing in our nation's capital. I enjoyed the city, and I felt very American and very patriotic. After that, we ended up in New York City in time to see the Empire State Building on a very smoggy day and watch Princess Diana and Prince Charles' glorious and memorable wedding. I thought the marriage between Charles and Di was so *romantic* and perfect. I *loved* Princess Diana, and I later received a photo-graphic book about the details of the wedding. We watched the details of the story and felt excitement with a cloak of trepidation wrapped around it because soon we would be liv-ing there. I felt like I had a connection with Princess Di. While living in England and years later, I was bewildered to see the Royal marriage unravel. Later, on August 31, 1997, when the news reported her tragic death in a car accident, I cried al-most as though it was the death of someone I knew. Now the whole memory of moving to England is forever mixed with the royal event and story. It was almost surreal to watch the wedding on television in America (not real) as we knew we would be there in person soon (very real).

England is about an eight-hour flight from the east coast of the United States. It felt like we were up all night, but when we arrived at Heathrow Airport near London it was only 7:00 a.m. and we had a long day ahead of us. Because of the whole move details, we had our worldly possessions in nine suitcases (six people, remember?). Now what? Even though I'm sure Dad had thought about and figured out the details, I felt like he hadn't planned, and everything was unfolding as it was happening. We knew we were staying in a hotel a little while and staying in London but how on earth could we get six people and nine pieces of luggage out of the airport to the hotel? It was difficult because we didn't have enough people to carry all that luggage (two adults, two young teenagers, and two small children). I had a hard time carrying my suitcase. We took the subway (in London it is the Metro) from Heathrow to the city. Then after trekking through the myriad of escalators and confusing system to handle the multiple train platforms, my Dad figured out which train line we needed, and we knew that we would need to transfer at least once to get to where our hotel was. It was morning commute time, and it was comic when same said people and luggage tried to squeeze into a crowded train. A horrifying part was when we were getting off at a transfer station we almost were separated when some of us had gotten off, and some of us were still on the train, including my little sister. Somehow the closing doors reopened, and they could get off. All of us emerged from the dark subway station back out into the sun. It felt like a never-ending trek to get to the hotel because now we needed to walk a few large city blocks for the last part of the journey. At that point, I felt like my arm was falling off and I was so-o-o-o tired! Nonetheless, we made it. We managed to stay awake until 2 p.m. by sightseeing, then eating our breakfast and lunch. Then my parents acquiesced, and we went back to the hotel to take a nap. I remember that I still was soundly sleeping at 5:30 p.m. or so when someone woke me. I was amazed at how hard I had slept, but now it was time to go to dinner.

The rest of the story of living in England is another book, but the thread here is that two years went by and we finally learned that we were moving again. I had fully expected when I left California that we would be moving back. I was caught off guard to hear that we were going back to Colorado, not California. I felt devastated by this news. I gradually realized I wasn't going to see my friends from California again. Also, we were moving to a different area, and I would be in a high school different than where my elementary school friends were so I would be going through the whole new girl in school thing that I was so done with. Finally, I was going to have a tearful parting from the good friends I had made in England. In the end, our move to Colorado was the last of my "seven moves by the time I was sixteen" story. I have lived in Colorado ever since, almost 34 years now!

I think it is time for me to put this story to an end. I have realized that a lot of the "problems" I experience today are very like the stories about moving I include here. I frequently have 'new girl' feelings even with my friends today. It is time for a different perspective.

The way my parents interacted with each other was a dynamic in my family that affected my life. My Dad was intelligent, smart, solved the problems and handled the finances.

Even as an adult I strove to be like him and to impress him with my life. When I was in my forties, spending time with my Dad, I would struggle and feel like a little girl and get triggered so easily to the point that I would bite my lip and try not to cry. My Mom, on the other hand, was nurturing and caring and was amazing and tremendous at raising four children (frequently by herself). She helped me so much, many times in my life. She deferred to my Dad when it came to tough life choices and finances. Consequently, I saw a clear line in the sand that fed into my childish 'black and white' perspective. Men are smart; women are not as smart. Men are powerful and achieve what they want; women can't assert themselves, and they don't have what they want. When faced with a decision such as what to major in in college, Journalism or Engineering/Accounting, I felt as though I could not choose journalism and I needed to be more pragmatic and logical about how much money I would make. This way of looking at decisions worked, in that I did get a job, I could take care of myself, but it did not serve me because life is not black and white and making money does not always equal being happy.

"When I was in my forties, spending time with my Dad, I would struggle and feel like a little girl and get triggered so easily to the point that I would bite my lip and try not to cry."

I am fortunate to be where I am today. I had a career, and now I have a family. I can do things to challenge myself intellectually like writing and investing in the stock market. I don't blend my mind's black and white perspective with the nuances of a colorful world all the time, but at least now I'm aware and can at least talk myself through it. I strive to remember when I'm in the world that each person is operating from their experiences and I don't usually think of their perspective as being wrong, even if I don't share the same perspective. I haven't lived through their experiences. I love both of my parents. I understand it is not easy raising kids and they handled some remarkable things together. Over the years, I blamed my parents for any current day problems in my life, and now that I'm a parent, I can look back and see that I had a personality that factored into my perspectives and life lessons.

Chapter 2

WOMAN PLANS, GOD LAUGHS

*It is better to light a candle
than to curse the darkness.
— Chinese proverb often quoted
by Eleanor Roosevelt*

I went to Australia to visit my boyfriend Paul before Christmas 1999. It would be the first time we had seen each other since the beginning of November when he and I had said good-bye as he left on a six- month sabbatical to Australia and New Zealand. He had rented out his house, lent out his car to a friend, and had gotten a leave of absence from work. We had started dating at the beginning of July and our romance had blossomed quickly and wonderfully. I wasn't sure what was going to happen when he left the country for six months, but I knew I would miss him. We kept in touch by email the first six weeks of his absence. I hadn't expected what easy accessibility to email he would have there; frequently he found free internet cafes scattered around the country. Somewhere during those first six weeks we made plans for me to visit him in Australia for the New Year's Y2K celebration. I was excited to be with Paul but I wasn't expecting what happened. Australia has a huge elaborate firework show at the Sydney Harbor to celebrate New Year's. Paul took me to a romantic dinner and we took a walk underneath the Harbor Bridge. The Bridge was lit up with lights in a pattern which said Eternity. It was at this spot Paul asked me to marry him. I excitedly said yes! I was looking forward to my life with my soulmate and true companion. I came home from my trip as an engaged woman, ecstatic about my future life with Paul.

The year 2000 was starting off magically and special. I started the wedding planning process when I got back from Australia because we were planning to marry in September. We discussed our wedding and all the planning details by email while he was out of the country. I planned a second trip to visit Paul in March, this time to New Zealand. It was a fabulous trip! I was expecting Paul back from his sabbatical in the summertime, but he surprised me and came back early in April. Since his house was occupied and we were engaged, we decided he would move into my house. Now I was spending the fabulous summer with my future husband. Everything was going great!

The days flew by and soon it was August. Our wedding would be on September 3rd. Right around the very beginning of August I noticed blurry vision in my right eye. I could still see and read but it was like looking through a veil or white filter. Colors were not as vivid and I had problems seeing all the information on my computer screen. When I closed my left eye to put make-up on, my right eye could barely see well enough to discern how I was applying my eye shadow colors. I had learned make-up application techniques but I just hated that when I closed my left eye to apply the make-up I could not see how my left eye make-up looked especially while putting make-up on for the wedding. I had gotten Lasik treatment on my eyes in February to correct nearsightedness. People who have vision problems are ultra-aware of how they see. I had been extremely happy with my clear vision after Lasik. It was huge *always* to see, not just with contact lenses. So, I attributed the current vision problem to my Lasik procedure and the first doctors I saw were my ophthalmologist (medical eye doctor, not just vision corrections like an optometrist).

After frustration and multiple appointments where each doctor told me that my eyes looked good, I couldn't understand that there was no physical problem with my eyes. How could that be true, when I knew I didn't see clearly? Finally, one of the doctors had a frank conversation with me where he said, "At this point, I would recommend you see your primary care doctor who can explore medical reasons for your symptom." I could not comprehend what he had said. What kind of medical problems could cause me not to be able to see? Frustrated with my eye doctors, I called and made an appointment with my primary care doctor who I trusted and liked. I felt a sense of urgency to move through all options and determine the answer to why I couldn't see *before* my wedding. I wanted it completed so I could move on to my wedding and honeymoon with Paul, only three weeks away. My doctor examined me and asked about my symptom. She prescribed a medication to try and see if it helped. I got the prescription filled, got the medicine and followed the directions for taking it. After two weeks, I could tell it was having no effect and called her again. At that point, she said she was going to refer me to a neurologist to have an MRI (Magnetic Resonance Imaging machine—a fancy name for a scan that takes pictures in a different way than an x-ray). She mentioned the possibility of Multiple Sclerosis (MS).

I called Paul and we frantically searched the internet for more information on MS, which we thought we had heard about but didn't know much about. I wasn't angry or frustrated with anything or anyone, I was nervous. I was a "Design Your Plan, Take Action on the Steps of the Plan" person, and this was *not* in my plans. I struggled with what was happening. The information on the web was more frightening than helpful, as it always is if you're using it to be your own doctor. I had to call a specific hospital, which I was unfamiliar with, to schedule my appointment for an MRI. I mentioned my vision problem to my boss and the possible MS comment from my doctor to my boss, but I never talked about it again with her even when she later asked for an update. I simply said there was not an update and everything was fine.

I went to my MRI appointment during work and Paul met me there. The hospital admissions people helped me to know what I was doing. I had to sit with them as though they were going to admit me to the hospital and give them all my information including and most importantly my insurance information. Then they gave me directions to navigate the hospital for the Radiology department where the MRI people would be waiting for me. The technicians were friendly and polite but did not discuss anything with me except what my symptoms were and if I had any metal on my body (which causes problems inside the MRI machine, because it is like a magnet). I changed into a gown, took my shoes off, and secured my engagement ring in a locker. I would have to lie down for the test focusing on my head.

The MRI machine was large, with a tube in the middle of it. The neurologist had also ordered pictures with and without contrast dye. Apparently, he needed to be able to compare the two sets of pictures. I came into this with no knowledge, experience, or expectations. First, they had to put an IV (intravenous, allowing liquids, such as the dye, to go directly into the vein) in my arm. The poke was unpleasant but brief. Then they gave me rubbery ear plugs which they explained were needed because the machine was very loud.

I lay down on a narrow, bed-like structure. I was comfortable so far. I had a bolster under my knees, which felt strange and the technician put padding around my head and arms to keep me from moving during the testing process. While not having claustrophobia, thankfully, the testing made me feel uncomfortable and completely out of control. At least I was just lying down as if I was on the bed. Next, they explained what going into the machine would be like. I would be able to see up and into a mirror that showed a reflection looking outside the tube. The techs could talk to me and I could talk with them. Since I was ready, they pressed the buttons and the bed slid automatically into the tube of the machine.

The whole ordeal was crazy, weird, uncomfortable, and something no one should ever have to experience. I can't even describe how scared I was. These tests were all about *my* brain. Having a problem that required a special test to look at my brain to get an answer was terrifying. The questions the test would answer about the brain and intellect I had used my entire life were so scary to me, I wanted to scream! Short of a negative test result, how could any answer be a good one for me? The MRI machine takes pictures of what they call 'slices' of my brain. Then the 'layers' can be overlaid on top of each other to create pictures that kind of look like an x-ray of my head. I didn't understand any of this at the time and I only saw my pictures one time at my first doctor's appointment. However, all I knew at the time was that the technician would tell me how long the next 'pictures,' (aka brain scan) would be. He would say, "This first set will take seven minutes." I don't have claustrophobia, but this test could practically induce it in you. The angled mirror above my eyes was how I could 'see' the technician. Right now, I could see the technician behind glass in a separate room from the machine at a desk with a computer. Seven minutes didn't seem bad. I could handle that. I did wonder though, why the technician didn't stay in the same room with the machine but in the separate room with the computer. I was getting radiation! Imagine yourself in a tube with pressure around your head and sides, and then the scan starts.

The explanation of the machine being loud was like an understatement to me. The machine was loud enough to cause post-traumatic stress disorder and I learned that *seven* minutes could feel like hours. That was only the first picture. Each time the sound would stop and the technician would ask me how I was doing and if I was okay. "Yes," I squeaked, when I *wanted* to say was, "**Okay? Are you crazy? How is any of this okay? Nothing about any of this is okay!**" Then the technician said, "the next scan is five minutes". BEEP, BUZZZZZZZ, BRRRRR, BRR, BRR, BRR, BRR, BRR.

In some instances, the machine made a noise, CLOCK, TAP, CLOCK, TAP, CLOCK, TAP, CLOCK, TAP ... after forty minutes or so, which felt like *six hours*, I heard the technician explain I was going to come out so they could put in the contrast dye. Yay! I would see the outside office of the exam room, and instead of a tube with an angled mirror, I'd see a ceiling!!!!! The bed automatically slid out. I breathed deeply and enjoyed what almost seemed like fresh air. Then the technician inserted a syringe into my IV and I could feel the cold pressure of the contrast dye going into my vein. Ouch, now that hurt.

"Okay are you ready? The last scans will take about twenty minutes," said the technician. I meekly nodded, said, "yes" and adjusted my legs and knees on the bolster since they were getting sore. The bed slid in and I was squished and looking at the angled mirror again. BEEP, BUZZZZZZZ, BRRRRR, BRR, BRR, BRR, BRR, BRR. Silence for a few seconds, next scan CLOCK, TAP, CLOCK, TAP, CLOCK, TAP, CLOCK, TAP. I pictured my head surrounded by a gold aura and I imagined that God was protecting me. Finally, they completed the last scan, the bed slid out of the tube for the last time, and it was now the moment to get my bearings in an upright position, first sitting, then standing. I was thrilled to be out of the machine. I went to the changing area, got dressed, and put my engagement ring back on. The technician made sure to tell me that he would write his report of findings, send it to my doctor, and the doctor would call me with the results.

Wow, all that agony, and Paul and I just got back into our cars and went back home to wait by the phone for the results. I tried to relax after the testing since I did not have any news from my neurologist yet. Paul and I were uptight and worried, but we tried to go about the next few days as usual. I went to work, but I still had my annoying and frustrating vision problem that felt the worst when I worked on my computer. In the next day or so my neurologist finally called and set up an appointment to discuss the results. Paul and I were nervous and out of our element in the patient and caregiver roles. We intrepidly went to the appointment with the doctor to discuss the results. He was very somber, deliberate, and respectful. Could I say warm and caring? Not so much. The doctor said I had signs of MS but that the clinical definition required two distinct events and my optic neuritis was only one. Therefore, what I had was 'probable MS.' Then he showed me the MRI scan. It was quite scary for me looking at scans of my brain. The films looked just like an x-ray and he put them up on a lighted board so we could see through them. I could see my head and brain, which was weird and freaky by itself. Then he pointed out the white spots on my brain indicating damage from the MS. The dictionary defines multiple sclerosis as

> A chronic degenerative disease of the central nervous system in which gradual destruction of myelin occurs in patches throughout the brain or spinal cord or both, interfering with the nerve pathways and causing muscular weakness, loss of coordination, and speech and visual disturbances. It occurs chiefly in young adults and is thought to be caused by a defect in the immune system that may be of genetic or viral origin. (See Resources)

I describe MS as a disease of the central nervous system (CNS). The CNS is made of your brain and spinal cord. In

MS, the immune system cells, which typically fight disease, move from your blood and into the brain, so this is bad. The immune system cells now attack nerve cells and cause damage. The disease is progressive, which means it stays at least the same with existing damage, but typically gets worse over time and continues your whole life. Right now, we were looking at my brain in the early stages. I stared at the white spots and thought about what they meant. My brain and my intelligence were a huge part of my personality and life as I knew it. I already felt like I couldn't handle having something wrong with me. As I understood more and more about what was wrong with me I felt attacked. I felt stalked by this mysterious disease personally, as well as if my personality, my career, and everything I knew was under assault. I was devastated and frightened.

We discussed a research study called CHAMPPS, which had ended with the results recently published. In it, patients with 'probable MS' had been started on treatment with a medicine called beta-interferons or another drug called glatimer acitate (Copaxone). The study data showed that it was important to start patients on treatment right away and not wait for a second symptom to appear; the belief was that MS would continue progressing in the interim. I was stunned and struggling to understand all the new information I was learning. Now looking back, I can understand that I was lucky because people like me, diagnosed in 1990 instead of 2000, had no treatment options available to them. I was grateful that it was now 2000, I had been diagnosed relatively quickly meaning I wasn't being bounced from doctor to doctor struggling to learn what was wrong, I could be started on medication right away, and I wasn't having symptoms related to walking. By the way, the medicines we're talking about can only be taken through an injection. I do not mean going to the doctor's office and getting an injection by a nurse or doctor. I had to learn how to inject myself to take the medication. The doctor gave me information packets on the two drugs (which included a video demonstration!) to take home and think about and discuss with Paul. I was comparing a drug called Avonex to a drug called Copaxone. I asked if I could take the drug while I was trying to get pregnant or if I was pregnant. The answer was no because pregnant women had not participated in the drug studies. With animals, there were not good outcomes and so it was recommended *not* to take the medication if you wanted to get pregnant. We agreed to follow up after my wedding and honeymoon, which was a relief to me. I wouldn't have to think about it for a while.

What do you do when your world turns upside down in a matter of weeks? How does one process this? Paul and I talked and discussed it. I told him I was sorry I had been diagnosed with MS and asked him if he still wanted to marry me. He said of course he did and no he wasn't mad at me; it wasn't my fault. He said he loved me and I shouldn't be sorry. It was a painful burden for both of us to bear because the future with MS is unknown. We were struggling to understand what MS was, and we were not even sure how to process, deal with and plan for this news. We were largely naïve and very optimistic about our future and wanted to proceed with our planned lives.

Then I started sharing the information with my family and friends. That is the start of a horrible process. You see how strong people are and how well *they* can handle real problems. People reacted by denying and arguing with me that it couldn't be true because no one else in our family had it. A lot of hope was placed on the slight chance that I would never have another event and so never really have MS. Telling my friends was a lesson that showed who your real friends are. Most people either had no response or avoided the truth because they didn't know what to do. A few friends would later support me by raising donations and walking with me in the Annual MS Walk put on by the National MS Society. I chose not to tell anyone in my work life. I felt like it was detrimental to my career for people to have any question about my mind and my abilities since it was such an important part of my work. I even told informed friends in my network not to mention it to anyone and to treat it as private. Many of them couldn't understand why I was concerned, but I dreaded and feared the accounting community who knew me having any doubts about my abilities. One of my family members was very shocked that I wasn't sharing it with everyone I knew because that is how she would have handled it herself. What I learned quickly was that this was my cross to bear and that no one could help me with that. It is different than with a disease like cancer, which is terrible news but for many there is a process to recovery for people to hang on to and to get help with. MS is a life-long disease with no cure. The diagnosis happens and then life moves forward just like it does for everybody. The huge unknown of what any of it would mean to me and Paul's life was a burden only we could bear and only we understood on an emotional level.

People can die of MS complications and MS could affect any possible part of one's body, skin, muscles, touch senses, equilibrium, coordination, spinal cord and walking, mind and thinking, swallowing, and other things I'm sure I'm missing. Still, people with MS typically die of other causes in the same percentages as the regular population by age. Heart disease, accidents, cancer, and other diseases can be the reason for death for people with MS just like anyone else. If nobody knows the future and there is a huge variety of ways to leave this earth, what is the real difference for people with MS? We have the gift of carrying the burden of the labeled unknown which we can't predict, and we live with that knowledge in our consciousness. Everyone else has unknowns that will happen but they can ignore them and keep them out of their mind because things *usually* work out. Almost everyone *will* have a loss when they age or when they lose someone. Each day is important and *now* is the only moment we have. Projecting into the future and planning to have love and happiness when we get to a certain point later doesn't work for me. Looking back and being critical and unforgiving of myself in the past keeps me from being aware of and living *now*. I didn't know how to do this before MS, and I do still struggle at certain times. But I now know to take each day as a gift because it is. I know to appreciate my mobility because I have it *now*. I love and recognize my family as an incredible gift in my life. I am grateful that God gave me a wake-up call from my old perfectionist focus on worldly concerns. I dabbled with the idea of being a writer for years, but for me to voluntarily take the leap away from my familiar corporate career to the unknown of something else somehow seemed impossible for me to do. The Universe nudged me in a different direction at various times, which I ignored. Only MS could shove me from my deeply imbedded and learned habits. In that context, I am grateful for my MS. I am also grateful for my husband who helped me to change when I needed to and who changed with me. He stepped up when I needed support financially because that was part of what these changes would mean to us.

"If nobody knows the future and there is a huge variety of ways to leave this earth, what is the real difference for people with MS? We have the gift of carrying the burden of the labeled unknown which we can't predict, and we live with that knowledge in our consciousness. Everyone else has unknowns that will happen but they can ignore them and keep them out of their mind because things usually work out. Almost everyone will have a loss when they age or when they lose someone.

Paul and I got married on a perfect fall day in the Colorado mountains with an outdoor ceremony. The deer even made an appearance for guests and family before the ceremony started on the grass pasture on the mountain slopes. We could see it from an outside balcony where we got married. The ceremony was beautiful and designed by Paul and me. Our good friends and family did readings and we had an Indian smoke ceremony to acknowledge non-traditional spirituality since we were outdoors and I was so happy to be married to Paul. The food was delicious and we had fun seeing our friends and family. I danced with Paul to Mark Cohn's "True Companion" for our first dance. I am glad and grateful I also danced with my Dad. I was honored to have my father and mother there

"Projecting into the future and planning to have love and happiness when we get to a certain point later doesn't work for me. Looking back and being critical and unforgiving of myself in the past keeps me from being aware of and living now."

even though they were now divorced. They walked me down the aisle together, which is a moment I'll never forget. The day was perfect and when the Purple Plymouth Prowler pulled up to the building and surprised me, I was excited and knew I was starting a great new life. Paul drove us to a hotel for our wedding night and I felt blessed! A few days later we went to Estes Park for our honeymoon where we stayed for a week. The fun and adventure just went on and on and on. It was a wonderful and romantic send off for the beginning of our marriage!

This book explains some traumatic events with getting diagnosed with MS. Of course, the journey is not over yet. I will share some other stories of life where I couldn't control the outcome as I have previously in my life. There are many other sad stories about what it is to live with MS. My message for you is that although I am stubborn and I learn slowly, I've gotten to a great place in my life. I can see that while I needed to process the predicaments in this book the way I did, there are other ways to handle these types of situations. I experienced real pain with the calamities I'm sharing, but I am learning that I caused some of my pain with my high expectations. Going with the flow and moving forward with my unplanned reality would give me more joy on a minute-by-minute basis (I didn't believe this could be true!) I have gotten to the point where I am better at living in the moment. I acknowledge myself for all the things I *can* do and the *gifts* I have. I am no longer in a pit of despair and I am enjoying my life. I know that God is taking care of me and I'm here for a reason and I'm here to share these stories for the people who need to hear them. The great thing about it is He is walking with me and is not going to give up until I reach my full potential.

Each day is important and now is the only moment we have."

Chapter 3

The Intellectual Fallacy

*It's being willing to walk away that gives
you strength and power—if you're willing to accept
the consequences of doing what you want to do.*
— Whoopi Goldberg

I was surrounded by intellects growing up. By that, I mean that people were intelligent and smart. My Grandpa DuMond, my father, his brother and sisters, and many cousins. Among this group, the core belief was that all things could be analyzed and solved. My Dad was an engineer in the Air Force; solving problems is what they did. When we would play Scrabble, there was always the best and right solution. We would have great discussions and solve the world's problems around the kitchen table. Somehow things seemed logical and easily managed and understood so I always believed things would work out well and no problem could be unsolved. It is a very secure feeling when you're in that place. You're smart enough for anything. Your brilliance will ensure your protection from risk and not only can you solve your own problems, but you can also help other people solve their problems.

I was an auditor; the perfect career for this mentality. In the auditing world, I was to go to a company, look at their books, and put on my "what could go wrong" hat. Auditors look at all the possible scenarios where the books could be wrong, where things aren't as they appear, and test those things by looking at objective evidence to prove that those facts are indeed correct. I loved to pull out my bag of tricks when someone described a problem they were having. Those tricks were all the intellectual knowledge I had to help people solve their problems. I would suggest things I knew about insurance or finance to help them solve the problem.

Intellectual people have a lot of knowledge and read a lot of books. It is meaningful to know the history of the world and mankind. With that knowledge, great discussions and debates can be had to take the world's problems and tie them up in a bow. I used to love to listen to my father explain politics or problems and then methodically apply logic to them to come to a solution. He seemed brilliant to me. Now my brother Don does similar things. It is eerily familiar when he is in that mode. Nevertheless, being intellectual doesn't solve the world's problems, because these people aren't necessarily the ones in a position to change anything or solve anything on a grand scale. I notice this intellectual fallacy whenever ordinary people have any political debate on a world problem over dinner or drinks. No matter people's opinions, they will provide the support to prove what they believe intellectually or to disprove the other side of the debate. There was a certain hunger for this stimulating conversation in my family, especially on my Dad's side. On radio and television, you hear discussions about taxes, fiscal policy, the country's budget, laws that exist or laws that should exist, inflation, or the future price of gold. You may hear what the tea party is doing or what the Occupy movement is all about.

My life experiences have taught me that my intellect couldn't always help me or solve all my problems. I thought I was protecting myself and managing my risk through financial decisions I made (like buying life insurance), but I still got MS. The intellectual skills that I so admired seemed to fall flat when I felt alone. Paul and I struggled to know how to deal with my problems. For example, an exasperating problem I dealt with is when I kept losing my keys and was unable to find them quickly on my way out of the house. I would frantically search through the house looking for them, scrambling room to room and floor to floor before ultimately finding them and leaving stressed out and late. We used analytical skills to brainstorm solutions. The cause of the problem was that I would put my keys down wherever I happened to be and because my memory was affected, I forgot where I had put them down. We put up a key organizer by the door for entering and exiting. We put a spare pair of car keys for each of our cars on the organizer. They could be used temporarily in emergencies. I started leaving my keys in one set place on the counter by the door first thing when I came home. It took a great effort for me to build the habit even though it sounds relatively simple. Eventually, we handled the chaos most of the time.

Another problem I have that can derail me is leaving and going to a meeting. My Women's Investment Club meets once a month. Each meeting I must bring information related to the stock I'm watching, plus I usually have another job. Right now, I'm the President, so in that duty I bring the agendas and am prepared to run the meeting. Again, relying on my intellectual skills, I realized I need to get my things ready early without time pressure and organize them before I walk out the door. I function best when I don't wait until the last minute or leave in a time crunch. Many people probably relate to this and have had to learn this to function well in their lives; what makes this different is that my lack of organization is an MS symptom. I used to be able to handle the pressure quite well in my opinion. I considered myself as functioning best with some amount of stress, and I even sought it out. Now, I must conscientiously plan not to have the stress and even baby myself to function at the level I want. Otherwise, I will be out the door having forgotten one or more of the items I need. I've learned this the hard way many times. Now, I start working on what I need to do the week before and start to get my items ready well before I need to. In that way, I can use my intellect to compile the stack I need to take with me the day before. This strategy has helped me be successful and relaxed before I leave and once I'm there.

From a young age, I would assess whether I was "okay." "Okay" meant that I could take care of myself, and I could handle life without my parents' help. As I grew and matured, I always came back to this self-assessment repeatedly. Finally, as an adult, I knew I could take care of myself. I had a job, I could pay bills, I had a life with friends, and I suspected that I might have it figured out even better than my parents did. I lived in this bubble a long time. For me it was the bubble burst when serious things went wrong like the year I learned about my MS disease. No amount of intellect could prevent a medical problem. My stronghold coping skill of intellect couldn't prevent my illness. I couldn't take the unknown future of such a disease and figure out anything to protect myself or to calm myself.

My natural mode of analyzing and assessing felt hollow. I looked to my family history to explain why I had this disease. There was no known prior history in my family. I looked for other risk factors and that didn't help either. Living in Colorado, 1 in 500 people will get MS. Ok, great, analysis done, but that didn't move me forward or help in anyway. Latitude of where you live is a risk factor. The closer to the equator you are the less risk, the further away you are, the greater risk. That was confusing. I was born in California which is low risk, but we moved and later lived in England and Colorado which is high risk. There is something magical about the age of fifteen. If you move from low risk to high risk after the age of fifteen you will adopt the risk of the high-risk area. So, when I moved at fourteen from low risk California to high risk England where I turned fifteen, followed afterward by a move to high risk Colorado, that was not favorable for avoiding the disease of MS. However, my brothers and sister made the same moves I did and they don't have MS. There is no intellectualizing such a diagnosis. As my auditor friend used to say, "It is, what it is..." The shock and trauma I experienced after my diagnosis, the fear for my unknown future I felt, and the realization that I couldn't control and minimize risk against everything was a painful time. I dealt with this by finding a therapist, Patricia Daily, I completely trusted and with whom I could feel safe to discuss all the intricacies of the impact of this illness on me and my new marriage.

Do you remember after the 9/11 attacks in 2001? Did you notice the fear and shock of people everywhere that such a disaster could happen here in America? Such an unimaginable tragedy was not supposed to could happen to us as Americans, right? I remember seeing society's reaction and thinking how now everyone was feeling the shock and trauma that I had been feeling since my diagnosis in 2000. Only I'd been feeling mine in isolation and now the whole country was feeling it. I know my MS diagnosis is different from the terrorist attack that happened on 9/11, but the reactions and emotions around me mirrored how I felt almost exactly. People didn't know what to do with themselves. Should they go to work as normal? Should they ever fly again? My husband and I had bought and built a new house in a new neighborhood. When I was first married and Paul was traveling, I'd be home alone and I enjoyed watching planes flying through the night sky out the back window. I remember looking at the planes and feeling very much in love with Paul and giddy happiness for our decision to buy our house. Paul was working in California when 9/11 happened. I don't know if you remember, but planes were grounded for several days. Because of that he couldn't come home for a week and he stayed in California and visited his parents in Grass Valley. In the days after the attack, the night sky was empty of planes and their lights. It was lonely, eerie, and strange and empty. That is the feeling I had after my MS diagnosis.

I always thought I could rely on my intellect and knowledge to make life go well for me. I was well educated, I had traveled to Europe and Australia. With the amazing knowledge, I had gained in my life, I figured I could plan and live my life from that place. I thought that when things had gone well, such as getting my degree, getting a job, and living on my own, that I had done something right and that I had figured it out. Because I had these experiences I believed I must be correct. My world turned upside down beginning when I found out I had MS. Many of the stories you'll read in this book are of things going wrong and being outside of my control. Because my intellect was not helping me deal with the loss of my health, when my pain was so great and I could hardly leave the house, I continued to go to church. In fact, I started going more frequently. Later, I talk more about spiritual growth. I began spending more time in prayer and leaning into the Lord and working on my spiritual growth. Because of this I had plenty of time for everything to heal. I experienced these results because of spending the time doing this, the opposite of intellectualizing.

I used to be an expert at thinking and analyzing. It is common in my family to discuss a problem or topic to "see if we can figure it out." I always thought there was a combination of solutions and ideas that could unequivocally solve the problem. Solve meant 1) make the problem go away, 2) lessen the emotional discomfort or pain and 3) protect yourself from ever having that problem again. These three points were with all one's heart the way I designed and assessed my progress in life. I thought there was beyond question a way I could achieve these three things if I just used my thinking and my brain well enough. Now it seems like the three things are meaningless and that I was asking the wrong questions.

Life is a lot of things but being able to protect yourself from everything you get afraid of is an illusion. Life is more about learning not to live in fear. Life is about asking "What is this problem telling me about my life?" Life is a journey and dance. If a disease like MS changes your health, how do you design your new life going forward? How do you make the most of the situation? Eventually you move forward and live your life with intention, designing the world around you with your choices, attitudes, and beliefs.

Having MS and having my symptoms, impaired cognitive reasoning and memory, impaired word-finding skills and vision problems creates a perfect storm for someone like me. In my life, I've valued the attempt to be perfect. I thought it was realistic to do many things at one time and to expect to do them well. My peace of mind and contentment came from scanning the different areas in my life and seeing that they were under control. When things go out of control, what now? I do have problems, I do make mistakes, there are things about myself that I don't see. I received an email one day from a close friend. We were planning to have lunch. Late the night before, I realized I wasn't sure of the location of where we were supposed to meet. Patting myself on the back for remembering to follow up and take care of this detail or problem, I sent my friend an email asking, "which location of Qdoba?" Later the next day when I checked my email, I had a response from my friend that said, "Do you mean Panera? It is at Southwest Plaza." I was quite horrified to realize that my

> "The values that you hold dear are the very ones that get questioned on a life journey, if you live long enough.

memory had not been accurate at all about our previous conversation. As a result, my question made no sense and made it seem like I wasn't all "there." Her response was polite, not pointing out my error, and allowed me to be dignified in my reaction and to move on. This example is a small thing. No one should get upset about forgetting the details of a conversation or appointment. However, it is one way that MS has affected my life. I've had to learn not to worry so much about my image as I did in the past since I might not look like I have it all together. My symptoms can make me appear flustered and not smooth. Precisely my Achilles heel! I've had to learn to let go of my crazy perfectionism, another blessing from God. My weakest vulnerability (my image, what other people think of me) is exactly the problem God gave me to deal with. With this path, I will deal with it repeatedly until I can finally relax and let it all go. The values that you hold dear are the very ones that get questioned on a life journey, if you live long enough.

Chapter 4

TREATING MY MS

Most people are about as happy as
they make up their mind to be
— Abraham Lincoln

After we got home from our Honeymoon and back to work we dutifully watched the videos about the medications that I had discussed with the neurologist. Copaxone was a daily injection. Avonex was a once a week injection. I chose to start my medication therapy with Avonex strictly because it was less invasive and had fewer dosing times to follow. The problem with doing self-injections for treating MS, among other things, is that it interrupts your life and makes you think about how you have MS. A once a week interruption is better than a daily interruption, in my opinion. A nurse came to my house to train me. I had asked Paul to be there too. The administration of the drug is simpler now, but when I first started taking medication the medicine came in two vials (glass bottles with a rubber top) that I had to mix. One vial had sterile (very clean) water and one vial had concentrated, powdery medicine. I had to use a new syringe to extract the water from the water vial and move the syringe to the medicine vial, put the needle on the syringe through the rubber top and gently push the water from the syringe into the medicine bottle. It was important to go slowly and to gently shake the medicine bottle to mix it as the water was going in. TAH DAH! Now I had a vial of the medicine I needed for my injection. The nurse had practice aids for me to inject before I injected myself. I used only water for the 'test' injections. The process seemed easy but the syringe needle was long and sharp. Essentially, I don't know how I stuck the needle all the way to the muscle in my thigh. Once the needle was in, I slowly injected the medicine from the syringe. Then I was done. The challenge was always the initial poke. Because the needle was long and scary, Paul came up with the idea of putting on my favorite Sting CD; I could listen to a song that made me feel relaxed (I just happened to like Sting pun unintended).

More women than men get MS; the ratio is 2 to 1. It is fortunate that successful disease-modifying treatments for relapsing/remitting MS exist now. Although there is nothing they can do to cure or prevent MS, the disease-modifying treatments have slowed successfully, the progression of my MS. I followed my neurologist's advice and went on treatment right away. MS can strike at any age, but the age group for those first diagnosed is usually within the range of 20 to 40.

At the time of my diagnosis in 2000 there were three disease-modifying drugs, as I've described. In 2017, there are thirteen or fourteen drugs that treat relapsing/remitting MS. I'm fortunate to have had good medical care here in

Colorado. I benefitted from having the best neurologists who were current on the various drugs there were to choose from and who assessed whether the drug I was on was effective at managing my disease course. Also, when my doctor was Dr. Ronald Murray, a renowned neu-

"I do feel supported by the Holy Spirit and that I'm being led to the right decisions for me."

rologist who was involved in several clinical trials, he told me about them and I could get involved and vary my treatments accordingly. Over the years, I've taken Avonex, Copaxone, Rebif, Tysabri and Aubagio. These changes have been important because I have been able to tell that cognition problems I had earlier in my disease course have gotten better as my neurologists changed their recommendations and prescriptions, thus using different drugs. My MS has been stable for many years, which is the best outcome you can hope for with this disease. It is an unquestionably good outcome and allows me to live my best life.

Undoubtedly, the bummer about the typical age of diagnosis for women affected by MS is that they are usually during their childbearing years. As I've covered already it is not recommended to take MS medication while trying to get pregnant or while pregnant. So, one way or another it pits the decision to have a family against treating your disease. Part of my story, which made a challenging situation even more challenging, was that I was already older than average when I was trying to get pregnant because of the timing of meeting my husband. For a little over a year after my diagnosis and our marriage, my husband and I put off having a family to treat my MS. I believe that treating my disease first and along the way when I wasn't pregnant has made me able to live a whole and happy life.

Many people have had long term success with Copaxone, and my doctor prescribed that later, when I wasn't trying to get pregnant. Copaxone was the drug that required self-injection seven days a week. MS is a unique disease from individual to individual. My symptoms can vary immensely from someone else's. Copaxone was the least favorite drug of any of my treatment plan mainly because it is hard work to self-inject yourself for seven days in a row, then start the process over again. I consistently had painful, red injection site reactions. There are seven distinct injection sites, on the back of either arm, right or left upper thigh, left or right back hip, and finally, stomach. You were also supposed to rotate in a circle at each injection site so you weren't reinjecting in the same site seven days after you had previously injected that site as this can cause skin problems. It would have been difficult for me to stay on Copaxone long term for many reasons though I suppose I would have tried if I was modifying the disease course successfully. After ten months on the drug, however, my doctor ordered an MRI and learned that my MS was active, meaning the drug wasn't working. He changed my drug to Rebif at that point. That change was a relief and blessing in several ways.

Rebif had a better self-injecting profile because it only required three injections per week. The drug mechanism was a betainterferon1a, and it worked differently than Copaxone. I stayed on the drug for a couple of years and it worked well for me during that time. I may have stayed on it longer except one of the side effects of this drug is that it can cause depression. I went off Rebif to try for baby number two, but I genuinely shy away from that depression side effect! MS is hard enough without also having to deal with depression at the same time.

One of the more interesting stories about my treatment happened when Dr. Murray told me about a clinical trial he was doing. In this trial, they were comparing the drug Tysabri between two administration courses. The first option was the typical way the drug is administered, by infusion in the hospital compared with the second option, which was an intramuscular injection in the leg. Tysabri is one of the most effective drugs for Relapsing/Remitting MS, but it also has a risk of developing Progressive multifocal leukoencephalopathy (PML), a rare and usually fatal viral disease. I had been interested in taking the drug because of its excellent efficacy. Although I felt daunted by the risk of a fatal side effect, participation in the study was appealing to me because I would be under a doctor's supervision while taking the drug.

I moved forward with the study and took Tysabri by injection for the length of the study, which was eight months. My health was strong while taking that drug, and I felt as though my cognitive symptoms and even my vision improved. After the study, I started to take Tysabri by infusion, the typical manner. The infusion lasts an hour and then you are supervised by the nurses for another hour. Treatment occurred every 28 days, so once a month. I had been experiencing injection fatigue. It was such a relief to have "me time" at my monthly appointments and finally to stop with self-injections. I took the drug for four and a half years and it was by far my favorite. Sadly, I experienced an allergic reaction the day after an infusion and I had to stop taking the drug. The Universe was letting me know it was time to stop the drug. It was sad news because it was my favorite drug, but it was good news because now I was off the drug that could cause a fatality. It was a strange experience, but I do feel supported by the Holy Spirit and that I'm being led to the right decisions for me in my treatment. I am thankful to my excellent physicians too!

After I had gone off Tysabri, I started taking a once daily pill Aubagio, which is the easiest drug I've taken. It has been over two years now and thankfully, my MS has been stable, thank the Lord!

Chapter 5
THE WORD I NEVER SAY

*Joy is what happens to us when we allow ourselves
to recognize how good things really are.*
— Marianne Williamson

I have been successful in my life. I credit that trait to lessons my father taught me and the way he lived his life. I learned from my parents and understood what it took to be successful in school from an early age. Once I felt like I understood that concept, I just went about the work of doing it. I went to school for two years overseas and it was completely different than my education up until that point. So, I repeated the process. I figured out how the new school system worked and what it took to be successful. Then all I had to do was do it. I had some help from my parents at that time, because they provided a tutor for my French classes, which I was very behind in. In college, I studied to get an Accounting degree (after a long process to figure out that was what I wanted to do). I had written a paper in college about jobs in my field of study where I interviewed someone working in a Public Accounting Firm. Then, at CU Boulder I saw something about a Business Fraternity meeting called Beta Alpha Psi. The person I had interviewed for my paper had mentioned that joining that group was an important step in getting a job in Public Accounting. I went to the meeting, met people, and networked and then became a member. Later the Public Accounting Firms came to campus to interview people, and I received a couple of job offers. By the time I was 23, I was working for a big four accounting firm called Ernst & Young. I had learned and internalized that I oversaw my life and I was somehow commanding good outcomes.

I worked at that company for five years, leaving when I was twenty-eight. That was the first time I looked up and around and started living a balanced life, with a career and a personal life. At times in that process I met people who were getting married and were married. A serious relationship at the age of nineteen burned me. I knew I wanted to be married and to have a family, but I was very committed to standing on my own two feet. At a young age, I had done some thinking and wanted to have kids someday but I thought it would be when I was older, say twenty-five. When I hit that birthday, I thought about this and realized I am not 'older;' that was a silly goal I had. Once I was out of my Public Accounting job, though, I saw the possibility of eventually having a family.

Then logistics and my problem-solving method settled in: I would need a husband for this to happen! I dated and was very active and I had good friends. I even joined a 'singles' club. The format of the club was great. You weren't paired up with someone, but the club published a monthly activity calendar. It was natural for me because I navigated towards activities and adventures I liked. I met a lot of people including good women friends. I have stayed friends with some of those women for years. I did meet people to date, but mostly it was fun to just be with the group. There was not quality husband material in that group for me during that time.

I did have a long-term relationship with someone who I had fun with, but I would often think, "If he proposed, what would I say?" It didn't take much time for me to realize I did not see myself thinking "Yes." We ended up breaking up. We had spent a lot of time together and it was quite a painful break-up. At first, I was mad that I had spent one year with the wrong person. Then I settled in and accepted myself as I was. I was joyful and appreciated all I had, which was a lot! I felt I was in a great place and I was at peace. I decided to be happy to be single.

Two months after my break-up I ran into someone who *used* to be in the singles club. I had met this person several times at various parties. It was Paul! Lots of people called him Woody (for his resemblance to Woody Harrelson on the TV show *Cheers*). I had always found myself gravitating toward him when I had first met him. I would be at a party with my then boyfriend (who had introduced me to Paul originally) and I would be a bystander to Paul's conversations with others. What I liked about him was he was very good at listening to other people and being very thoughtful about his interactions with others. I found myself remembering all this every time I happened to be in the same place he was. Well now, I was running into him as a single woman who was in a pretty confident place. I had a misconception at the time that he wouldn't want to date me because I had previously been dating his friend. I talked to him that night thinking he darn well better want to date me! Well, when you're thirty-two and you meet someone and you're in the right place you know yourself better than you did when you were younger and you can learn things about the other person more quickly than before. I knew Paul was a good thing and it seemed to be mutual. We went on a group biking and hiking trip in July, one date after that and the rest is history. We continued to date and enjoy ourselves.

One of our dates included dinner out and the place we were eating was near a little Lake with a Gazebo. Now, many years later I don't remember the place or the food, but I remember the company and the conversation we had that night. After dinner, we took a walk outside and we found the Lake which had a path around it. We decided to walk around the lake. The path led to a gazebo where we stopped to enjoy the quiet and look at the view. I was standing facing out on the gazebo leaning on the rail and Paul walked up behind me, putting his arms around me. He started talking about our future family, which surprised me. I had gotten used to dating men that never talked about the topic of a family. Paul continued and described how we would have two kids and that they would both be boys. I had to stop him then and tell him, "You know that you can't guarantee that they would be boys, don't you?" We continued to talk about having kids on our walk. I told him that I could see myself having two but that there was a possibility of having three. He didn't agree because then the children would outnumber the parents. I hung on to my thought for a long time.

As you've read, Paul proposed to me in Sydney, Australia. Paul and I loved spending New Year's there, the fireworks show was phenomenal and very impressive. Paul didn't propose then, he did it when the *proposal,* not the *fireworks,* was in the spotlight. On January 2, Paul asked me to be his wife and I happily said yes! Our theme for our wedding was *Together for Eternity* because I truly believed we were meant to be together and that I had found my soul mate.

* * *

Paul and I decided not to try to have children the first year of our marriage. We wanted to enjoy being together and it seemed like going on medication right away was the best thing for me and us. I started taking Avonex and stayed on my birth control pill. Our first year of marriage was great and we put aside the stress of the MS treatments and lived our life quite well during that period.

It was a year to fifteen months after we married that I talked to Paul about not wanting to wait any longer. I was now thirty-four and wasn't feeling so comfortable about waiting much longer to try to get pregnant due to my age. I also had a nagging fear that had been hanging over me my whole life. I had gotten my period right before I turned twelve and by the time I was thirteen, I was in painful agony with every period. All my mom knew to do was give me aspirin. Aspirin did nothing for the pain. After a while she took me to see a doctor who prescribed Ibuprofen. I started taking that which mildly helped the pain but mainly I learned to live with at least some pain each month. Eventually they came out with Naproxen Sodium (Aleve) and even now that is the only drug that works to relieve my pain. I always have one to two days during my periods that could take me out but usually I don't

Debie Monax

let it happen. On those days, I seek down time where I can use my heating pad and pamper myself.

Somewhere along my life path I was in a doctor's waiting room with time to read a magazine. On one occasion, I read an article that covered a variety of women's medical issues. One of the issues was Endometriosis. The word was familiar to me in some way and I didn't know why. I think I had heard the word at one of the early doctor appointments with my Mom. I read the article with great interest. Based on the symptoms described in the article, I had a suspicion that my painful periods were a sign that I had the *long word* disease. I put this idea out of my mind quickly. Worse still, the article included a strong implication that Endometriosis could cause infertility. Since I didn't know yet what Endometriosis was, and I wasn't married and trying to have a child, I couldn't comprehend what impact this would have.

The longest year of anyone's life is a year trying unsuccessfully to become pregnant. We had tried to get pregnant for a little over a year. I had heard of this book *Taking Charge of Your Fertility* by Toni Weschler. It taught me how to take my temperature first thing before getting out of bed. By keeping a chart of daily temperature, it was possible to predict ovulation and therefore the best time to have sex to conceive a child. I had never known any of this stuff, but now I was an avid learner. Nothing kills newlywed passion faster than the pressure to have sex on the three days each month that are best for conceiving. It was not always practical and it got less and less romantic each time you went through the process for the best timing. Paul frequently had to travel for work. He was always home for three-day weekends, but you never knew if the days he was gone were the ones when it could have happened. Then life went back to normal until it got closer to the end of my cycle. Maybe, just maybe, I wasn't going to have a period this time, and my temperature would stay high, which would mean I was pregnant. I bought the triple packs of home pregnancy tests, which always somehow ended up getting used up even though I never became pregnant. There was always the chance, right?

Recently, I found my charts in my bathroom drawer. They were neat with the name of the month on top, the temperatures charted carefully, and notes I had written for myself as instructed by the book. Notes about fertility signs, notes about what days we had sex, notes about the first day of my period. My chart looked normal just like the book as far as I could tell. Unfortunately, they all ended with the same conclusion: a couple of days where I spotted (not a great sign) followed by the drop-in temperature that occurs at the beginning of your cycle when you're getting and having your period. I had over twelve of the charts, and they all looked the same and made me sad. I remembered all the newlywed fun and bliss, all the hope and joy that we were trying, all the excitement that this could be it, all the planning life events where we weren't sure if I would be pregnant or not. We kept it up cycle after cycle until the sad days where you just didn't want to have sex because it was the days where you didn't need to and quite frankly you just needed the pressure to be off so you could get your sleep. I longed for the romance and fun of our early relationship and I longed for a baby and to begin the Parenthood stage of my life.

I thought you were supposed to give it a year before seeking help, but I found out later that since I was over 35 I should have sought help after six months. My doctor suggested laparoscopic surgery to assess any endometriosis and potentially clean up any adhesions. A laparoscope is an optic camera and tools which can be inserted into my belly button to "see" inside my abdomen.

I remember waking up from the surgery while still in that very groggy state and hearing a conversation that I couldn't completely catch or understand, but I had a bad feeling about what I was hearing. Now, I can't remember exactly, but what is coming to mind are words like "poor girl, she has adhesions everywhere..." I didn't feel good about it at all, and I had a recovery process to go through. My appointment to go over everything with the doctor was five days or so later. She surprised me when she explained my surgery and that I had Level IV Endometriosis. I was still trying to assimilate my diagnosis when she cut to the chase and gave me a business card for the Colorado Center for Reproductive Medicine (CCRM). She recommended that I continue to pursue my pregnancy desire using In Vitro Fertilization ("IVF")

The grief of not knowing if you ever will be pregnant is real pain and sadness, and people do not intend to be unkind. I realized it was not other people's business but I pretended to be cheerful and optimistic and not let the mask slip. Many of our friends were older when they got married and all had some level of difficulty having children. One by one, however, whatever the difficulty, it was overcome and eventually their baby was on its way. At times, it felt like everyone I knew was pregnant or had just had a little newborn infant that was with them every time we saw each other. Infertility is lonely and there is a lot of guilt in there. I asked myself things like "Why didn't I go to a doctor sooner?" or "Maybe there was something that could have been done earlier?" and "What was wrong with me focusing on a career?" I knew people who were having babies in their twenties and that seemed so young to me; I also asked, "Maybe I should have focused on getting married and having a family earlier and a career later?" I almost didn't believe how babies are made, but I always heard of people who accidentally and unexpectedly got pregnant; no there had to be some other trick or secret that I just didn't know about.

I felt like a failure at being a woman. The image of becoming pregnant easily became an expectation I put on myself. If instead I believed that whatever was meant to happen would happen and that there are many stories of what makes a happy family instead of one cookie cutter picture I would have been happier and enjoying my young marriage.

The word infertility seemed permanent to me. It is often used and spoken about with the doctors. I decided right away that I wouldn't say the word. If I was talking about any of the steps in our process I changed it to 'fertility problems.' Why call me infertile? I am a normal woman and I enjoy my femininity. These problems were related to the plumbing. The endometriosis had caused damage in my pelvis. At times in the infertility journey I felt alone and isolated. However, about ten percent of women (6.1 million) in the United States ages 15-44 have difficulty getting pregnant or staying pregnant, according to the Centers for Disease Control and Prevention (CDC). It was time for me to stop feeling guilty.

Chapter 6

THE MIRACLE OF SIERRA

Gratitude bestows reverence, allowing us to
encounter everyday epiphanies, those transcendent
moments of awe that change forever how we
experience life and the world.
— John Milton

I was off my medications while we tried to get pregnant on our own. Finally, we started the IVF process with CCRM in July 2003. We had already consulted with our doctor, Eric Surrey, about our case and my endometriosis. I had surgery with Dr. Surrey that April to close off my left fallopian tube. That was to keep toxic secretions from the endometriosis away from my uterus. If the secretions get into the uterus they alone can make it difficult for the uterus to support an embryo and pregnancy. I wasn't crazy about two surgeries, but I would do anything if I thought it was moving us closer to a pregnancy and a baby and I liked and trusted my doctor. The clinic was doing a clinical study on endometriosis and asked if I wanted to be a part of it. There was a financial benefit of

$1,000 off the cost of the procedure and the clinical benefit was modifications to the traditional IVF procedure that were considered specifically helpful to the concerns and challenges of pregnancy with endometriosis. So, of course I participated.

CCRM really have the process down and based on my menstrual cycle they completed a detailed calendar and protocol of each step in the process. It is complex and includes medication and hormones, syringes and pills, and its start date is based on the first day of your period the month before the embryo implantation will take place. I excitedly took my prescriptions to a specialty pharmacy that formulated specific medicines needed for the process. I came home with all my gear in a big paper bag.

The world doesn't stop around the dates of our precious IVF cycles even if they are of the greatest importance to us. We were planning on driving to Montana to visit my Mother and spending the Fourth of July weekend there. My siblings and their families were all going to be there too for an informal family reunion. The dates of my protocol had minimal medications before the first day of my period and some starting on Day 1 of my period which was probably going to be around the holiday weekend. I planned and brought everything I thought I would need on our trip. I got my period there and I wasn't supposed to take ibuprofen or naproxen sodium after Day 1. That was a problem because I managed my painful periods with these drugs. I remember that trip as a painful one, and I was anxious about the process and steps of the process that Paul and I were going through. The IVF process had become the center of the Universe to me, which seemed of little importance to the outside world. Pregnancy is the center of a mother's Universe, it's just that it is usually private. IVF made the process and the success of each step of the process more public than normal. I had to call the clinic and ask if I could take my normal pain medicine. They made an exception and gave me permission to take medicine. That helped my stress and comfort level immediately.

We were happy to get home from the trip to continue our IVF calendar protocol. Romance and making children didn't go hand in hand for us. It was medical and scientific, and it practically required business skills to keep up, ask the right questions, refill the prescriptions, and manage the financial side of submitting claim forms to insurance and tracking what had been paid or not paid. On the other hand, I see how lucky and blessed I was to be able to pursue this route to having a family. Paul's insurance covered much of the cost and we had the best doctors around right here in Denver.

The odds of getting pregnant with IVF, according to *Parent Magazine*, "9 Myths and Facts About Boosting IVF," are 41%. The statistics are continually updated and may be different at a center you are checking out. All kinds of factors affect those odds: whether you've been pregnant before or not, the age of the parents, family history, and on and on. From the standpoint of a couple experiencing infertility, it seems that a natural process like pregnancy is even more of a miracle than it already is. When you look at IVF as a process broken down into steps and odds of success, it makes the natural process of pregnancy seem more unlikely. The more I learned about the behind the scenes complexity of the process of getting pregnant, as you would only learn if you were at a fertility center, the more amazed I was at how anybody gets pregnant naturally. It is perfectly designed, almost engineered, but always with the powerful hand of God's involvement. I thought it was nothing to get pregnant, based on how easy it was for my mom to have four kids and my grandmothers before her to have a total of seven kids. It seemed like bread and butter. Meet the man of dreams, marry and soon there will be a hoard of children in the house.

Many of the IVF processes involve hormones which may be injections. The good thing about having taken MS medication by injection is that my husband and I felt well-versed in the process of administering them. One of the processes was taking oral medications (for both of us) and some were hormone patches. The gist of IVF is that the doctors mimic a super normal menstrual cycle and develop as many eggs as possible in the woman's body. Then on a specially calibrated schedule the developed eggs are removed from the mother's body through surgery. The eggs are fertilized with the man's sperm to create embryos that can be put back in the woman's body to continue to grow. Within days, a blood test can determine pregnancy and within weeks, an ultrasound can determine the details of the pregnancy and the baby.

The day of my blood test, I went in like usual for a blood draw. I went back to work. I got a call around 4:00 p.m. saying, "Congratulations, you're pregnant!" Paul was at work, too, waiting to hear the results. I called as soon as I had them and we were so giddy and excited. Our amazing dream had come true! We went out to dinner to celebrate, only I couldn't drink a glass of wine. I didn't mind at all. We went home that night with many thoughts twirling around in our heads and knowing how blessed we were!

I had started a project in June of painting the dining room of our house. I had designed it, picked out the paint colors, worked on the masking, and was working on the painting. The design was complicated with yellow on the outside sides of the wall around the archway entrance to the room and with green on the main walls in the room. The ceiling had a fancy and decorative stair-step design that was yellow on the horizontal sides that matched the ceiling and could be seen from below and green on the vertical sides to match the walls. I felt like I had made great progress, but we have high ceilings and my design included painting the ceiling. However, it turned out to be more difficult for me to paint than I had expected. I stopped painting for the IVF cycle and before our trip to Montana. After I was pregnant and things were going well, I had visions of me continuing and completing the painting project. I always thought I would continue all normal activity right up until the baby was born. But I went into the living room to paint once with my footstool to paint the high walls around the window sill. It was hot and each step was taking a long time, and I was getting exhausted.

Unfortunately, I didn't keep it up very long and I stopped. I talked to Paul about it, and he ended up being the one to finish the project. One of Paul's favorite phrases is that he bailed me out again. I loved being creative and it looks beautiful now, but I'm sure he would have been happier finishing a simpler paint project for me. I think this is a good example of how MS affects my life. I had great plans and set big goals, but being able to finish a big task like this is incredibly difficult for me. Although I was off MS medication now, there is a belief that pregnancy itself can be neuro-protective. The trouble comes in after having the baby when you can frequently have a boomerang effect and have an MS exacerbation. Finally, I picked out a floral fabric which had green and yellow colors in it because I decided to sew matching window coverings. I bought patterns and I sewed the curtains. Now it looks clean and stylish just as I imagined.

I worked at my Accounting job throughout my pregnancy. In a kismet sort of way, two other women at work were pregnant at the same time. One had a baby due in August, one in March, and my baby was due in April. It was great to have people to talk to day to day about various changes in our bodies and the amazing miracle of helping a new life grow. I signed up for an email that, based on your due date, sent me the daily development details and changes going on inside me. I enjoyed every change, and I liked to talk about it a lot. Looking back now, I notice that my perspective was slightly different than my two friends who were in their twenties and had gotten pregnant so easily. I was thirty-six when I got pregnant after years of trying and not knowing if it would ever happen to me. I remember talking with one of the women one day about the size of the baby's head and body. I was so amazed that it was possible for it to be true right in my belly that was getting bigger but still seemed like my tummy. She nodded her head and agreed with me, but her eyes glazed over because she wasn't as consumed with the details as me. She also had had serious morning sickness for twelve weeks or more, so she was hating certain parts about being pregnant. She wanted the baby but was not loving the pregnancy part. I on the other hand felt great and reveled in every detail of being pregnant. I had a theory that I had good genes from my mom and was meant to be pregnant a lot; I just had certain plumbing problems that made it more challenging for me to get pregnant.

I followed every rule about pregnancy. I knew everything to eat and everything to avoid. There is a wide spectrum of information on the health of the baby and the mother during pregnancy. I stayed on the most conservative end of the spectrum to avoid any possible food that had any risk at all, no matter how rare. I got looks all the time from people that hadn't heard the latest guidance or just thought I was kind of picky. I didn't care because this was my baby and my pregnancy. I knew the preciousness of it. I saw the beauty and I didn't take anything lightly. Paul and I were going to visit his Grandpa in Winnipeg, Canada by plane. When I asked the doctor about it, he said it was best for me not to travel by plane for the first trimester. We talked about it and decided to change the dates of our trip to later in my pregnancy even though it was hard to deliver the news to Grandpa Sid.

When we finally did travel, we spent a great time with Grandpa and we enjoyed it immensely. I also got to meet Paul's Canadian relatives most of whom hadn't been at our wedding. I only knew of them from the invitation and thank you card list. It was wonderful to finally put faces to names. Like most elderly people you meet, Paul's Grandpa has a beautiful story, and I'm so glad we got that time with him. He had been at our wedding and we celebrated his birthday with a barbecue at our house. He had worked for and retired from the Canadian Railroad for many years. I loved his gentle spirit, and I liked listening to his stories. One thing he talked about was his late wife Minnie. The two of them had sold their family home and moved into an apartment complex for people age fifty-five and older. It was going to be their time to enjoy the later years of life together surrounded by friends and the simplicity of not owning a house to take care of. When I met him, it had been ten years since she had died, and he loved talking about her and telling me their story. He was still sad that they hadn't lived in this new place very long before she died. Now he was living there but not with her. Maybe my memory of that moment is veiled by pregnancy hormones that made me soft and compassionate, but I don't think so. He was a great person and I'm glad I had married into the relationship.

During my very normal (to me) pregnancy I was on a normal three-week check-up schedule with my obstetrician. I learned later that as a high-risk pregnancy I should have requested more frequent visits. I had scheduled appointments as soon as I came back from the fertility doctor to go to my regular doctor. I had them all on my calendar, and I looked forward to them. I had been a manager for ten years and had employees who were pregnant. I had always been jealous that they had an indisputably valid reason just to pick up and leave work. In my serious way, I never took breaks from whatever urgent business there was. Finally, I was the one who could just leave to go to the doctor.

My birthday was February 7th, and I turned thirty-seven. My due date was April 19th. Our big work deadline was February 28th, not a problem, the baby wouldn't be here until after that. My calendar told me I had an appointment on February 19th. I went to work that day and left early for my appointment. I was feeling good, loved being able to tell the doctor how great I felt. He checked me out, agreed I was fine and I went home. My next appointment was scheduled the usual three weeks later. My husband and I had dinner and we went to bed.

Something woke me up in the middle of the night. I sat up in bed feeling a sharp pain on the left side of my abdomen just below my ribs, and I was feeling nauseous. I ran to the toilet and threw up. I was now completely awake. What was going on with me? I went back to bed, but my sharp pain was still there. Paul was 110% available when I was in pain and changed his schedule to help me out.

The next day I felt okay but did not eat much. I thought I'd had food poisoning. I went home that night and had a repeat of the night before. On Friday morning I felt fine again, but I didn't understand what was happening. I had not been nauseous my whole pregnancy. I was in my third trimester and had not heard of anyone being sick in their third trimester.

Friday night I felt badly again. Saturday, I continued to feel bad. I threw up with more frequency, and my sharp pain was almost always there. By Saturday night I was worried enough I called the on-call doctor. Paul took me to the hospital. I was surprised when they took me by wheelchair up to the 5th floor, the ob./gyn. floor, which was the same as where I had all my surgeries. They hooked me up to a monitor to listen and measure the baby's heartbeat. Until then, I hadn't worried about the baby because I felt it kicking and moving. I explained my symptoms, they drew some blood, and gave me some drugs that made me sleepy and able to eat some crackers and juice. By midnight they sent us home.

Saturday night I woke up in the middle of the night with pain and nausea and I threw up all the crackers and juice. I was angry because I couldn't believe I was still sick and they hadn't figured it out. I felt miserable all day Sunday and Sunday night. I told Paul that I was determined to be on the doctor's doorstep as soon as they opened Monday morning. Even though I had meetings, I called work and said I couldn't be there. Paul took me to the doctor's office where they were totally confused and didn't know what to do with me. No doctors were even there yet. One nurse was there to see me, and I knew her because I had seen her before. She gave me a very basic exam; asked me questions. Finally, she made the call that I needed to go back to the hospital. I am so grateful to her and know she went out on a limb without doctor's orders. She told me later that when she tested the reflexes on my knees, they were on fire, and based on that she knew I needed to get to the hospital for admission.

Paul and I were worried, but we climbed into the car and drove back to where we had been Saturday night. In an ironic turn, this second time at the hospital, I walked and took the elevator up to the 5th floor, no one offered me a wheelchair! This time the practice doctor was on call. She saw me and talked to me right after I got there. I was back in a maternity room wearing a monitor. She ordered blood work, but this time when it came back she had some serious news. I had something called HELLP Syndrome (hemolysis, elevated liver enzymes, low platelet count) and it meant I might have to deliver the baby early. According to the March of Dimes, HELLP Syndrome rarely occurs; one or two out of 1,000 pregnancies. I know this now, but luckily, I didn't know any of this in the moment.

I was stunned, sad, shocked, and confused. No, not me and not my baby! After all we'd been through so far! A perinatologist (a special obstetrician for high risk pregnancies) and my doctor came in to talk to us. The perinatologist seemed very concerned. He introduced himself, walked up, and sat on the edge of my bed. He explained that what I had was serious and dangerous for both the mother and the baby. He calmly and seriously said, "You must deliver ... **today**" With his words I stopped fretting and went into my "Do whatever it takes!" mode and Paul and I made eye contact as if, this was a serious quest we were starting.

The doctors started the steps of inducing labor. Paul and I called our families and got them up to speed. My mom made plans to fly out to Colorado from Montana that day. Prayers were being said for all of us all over the country as relatives got the word. Paul was with me for a meeting with the neonatologist (premature baby specialist) when she came in to answer any questions I might have. "Generally," she said, "thirty-two-week babies can do pretty well." She explained what would happen after they delivered the baby and how they would be examining it to determine what the next steps were. I asked her if I could put my baby to breast right away and if I would be able to hold my baby. She said that babies don't even know how to suck, swallow, and breathe until at least thirty-four weeks, so no, the baby wouldn't breast feed, and an exam of the baby and how it was doing would tell us if I could hold it or not.

Next, an anesthesiologist came by to tell me what my blood work was telling us about how we could manage pain. I hadn't decided how I wanted to do childbirth yet. I thought maybe natural would be okay if I had my mom's genes. Because of my low blood platelets, an epidural was too risky. As he ran through the list of other pain management options, all of which could affect the baby, the Universe decided for me. Of course, I was not going to make my preemie baby have any additional challenges (from drugs) and natural childbirth was what it was going to be. Paul was there for me and in agreement.

They induced me at 2:00 p.m. Paul and I talked and watched Seinfeld repeats and laughed. My delivery nurse was cheery and assumed that since it was my first pregnancy my labor would be long. I had to push the call button to ask her to come in and check me, since I felt that maybe I was like my mother and having a fast labor. I knew by her face that my labor was not going to be long. Then she said cheerily, "Well it looks like you're fully dilated, but since I need to get the doctor and neonatology in the room, try not to push yet!"

Paul and I held hands and took a deep breath. The whirlwind delivery process was starting where you know and feel the power of how much is out of your hands. Nurses came in, along with my doctor. Further back and away from the delivery table a crew of unknowns were there, though I didn't recognize them, my guess was that they were the neonatology experts. I felt relief to have all the right people there. Paul was next to me supporting me. I focused completely on following instructions. Bearing down to push seemed to come naturally. The baby was coming and I couldn't see anything. The baby came out and Paul yelled out, "It's a girl!" The nurses asked with surprise, "You didn't know already? It's a girl!" I felt love energy towards my little girl. I was anxious to know if she was okay. I heard crying and I was happy, because that seemed normal. After Paul had cut the umbilical cord, she was whisked away for her post birth tests and preliminary health check. I heard people talking but in normal voices. I was so excited that when they swaddled her and brought her to me to hold, I was surprised. The most beautiful baby on the planet's face was there in front of me. Paul and I were absolutely thrilled! I held her and talked to her; her eyes were closed again, and she looked peaceful. It was hard when they took her away after less than a minute and took her to the neonatal intensive care unit (NICU). Later I learned that she was 2 lbs., 13.8 oz. and 19 inches long. The doctors had guessed that she would be 4 lbs., but the HELLP syndrome had affected her growth in the womb and she was healthy but tiny. Then next thing I knew, I was in the room with just the doctor who was entering information into my computer chart. Paul had gone with the baby to the NICU, which gave me some solace that she was not alone, but it was so-o-o hard and unnatural.

Luckily, my phone rang, and it was my mother at the airport in Denver. She was anxiously wanting an update and was surprised when I said, "I just had her, she's here, it's a girl!" I told her everything had gone well and the baby seemed okay as far as I knew and that she and Paul were in the NICU. She was flooded with relief and excitement, and I was glad because she was on her way here. It was starting to sink in that they started the induction at 2 p.m. and at 6:02 p.m. the baby had arrived! I felt like I had set a record, all without medication. Then I called my sister and told her all about it. The rest of the family got calls after Paul had come back in the room. It had to be most exciting day of my life!

Paul and I decided to name her Sierra Frances Monax. My Grandmother's name was Frances and I liked that Sierra also had her name. It was funny, because we hadn't started deciding on names at this early stage, but we had decided that if it were a girl we would name her Sierra. We never could agree on a boy's name, which was now a moot point.

Paul was there for me while Sierra was in the NICU and I recovered. I couldn't walk for two days because of medication they had used. HELLP syndrome can be dangerous for mother and child. Once Sierra was born she was out of danger, but I was not out of the woods yet. Paul supported me emotionally when they took me to leave the hospital without my baby since she stayed in the NICU.

Both Paul and I visited Sierra in the hospital daily during her six-week NICU stay. Paul helped me deal with the planning and every three-hour pumping schedule I took up. I brought my breast milk for the hospital to feed Sierra while she was there since she couldn't breast feed.

I knew God was with me and I thought through all the amazing miracles in our story. We moved to the IVF path quickly. The sheer miracle of that process provided the embryos that became Sierra, and even though the reaction to my painful and mysterious symptoms leading up to the early delivery seemed slow, the right people were in place to give us good medical care and all went well. I felt like Sierra was a miracle many times over and she was certainly meant to be on this earth with us. I was immensely grateful for all that had happened. I was now a Mother, and I felt like I was embarking on the most important journey of my life so far. I just kept thanking God.

Chapter 7

BECOMING DISABLED

*You have to accept whatever comes and the only
important thing is that you meet it with courage
and with the best that you have to give.*
— Eleanor Roosevelt

In 2002, I was on a hiatus from accounting after leaving my last corporate job. One day the phone rang. It was a recruiter calling to speak with me about an Accounting Manager position he was trying to fill at a local company. They specifically needed someone who had knowledge of Statutory Reporting requirements for seventeen HMOs. I hadn't been seeking a job but this was synchronicity. The job sounded perfect, and it had come to me. I went through the somewhat rigorous interview process, interviewing separately with three different people. Their process seemed to take a long time. I finally received an offer and started work late October 2002. The pay was less than desirable, and I tried to negotiate a higher salary but then I accepted their offer, figuring I would see how things went.

One of the key skills I had when I started my new job at this insurance company was my knowledge of National Association of Insurance Commissioners (NAIC) reporting requirements for Statutory financial statements. I had been trained on them, had managed the accounting process, and prepared and filed them for years. I was an expert. Part of this process was undergoing Audits of financial statements. Audits were the true test of whether I had done the accounting correctly, understood the rules, and prepared the reports correctly. I had been responsible for the accounting department for two Health Maintenance Organizations (HMOs) at a time at my previous job. Various merger/divestiture activities had changed HMOs I managed. One of the achievements of which I was most proud was not having any audit adjustments because no mistakes were found.

These skills and job history may sound boring to you but it was the career I had built. Aside from my first job and this job, I was proud that I had maintained an extraordinary network of people in the Accounting world. I had worked for three different companies before this opportunity, and knowing someone had always gotten me in the door for an interview. I liked being the expert and the one with whom people would consult to get advice in this specialized area. The first performance review I received at the insurance company was very good, enough to get my annual salary to the point I had requested when I interviewed for the job. From that point on, I continued to receive increases annually.

The busiest time at work was December to February. We had to be prepared to close the books for the year ending December 31st. We worked under Generally Accepted

Accounting Principles (GAAP). Then we had to close the books in the first weeks of January and start the steps of preparing the NAIC (defined above) Statutory financial statements. The rules for Statutory accounting are specific to each state; thus, you need knowledge of each state's laws. The Statutory financial statements were due no later than February 28th.

One year, things were going along the same as in the past, except this time I was pregnant during this critical window of time. I wasn't concerned because my baby was due around April 19th. I felt good and we were at the point of filing our statements on time for February 28th. As you've read, I had to start my maternity leave early because my baby came prematurely, this year things went differently. The amazing team that I worked with completed and filed the statements on time of course, and honestly, for the first time in my life my attention was focused firmly elsewhere.

It was June before I went back to work, and I was dismayed to find out there were a few audit adjustments for calculations I specifically remembered reviewing. I had a sinking feeling that I had looked at them, and they were wrong but I hadn't detected those errors and corrected them. It wasn't that I never made mistakes but this felt like the core of my job and one of my greatest skills. Why did that happen?

I got dinged on my next performance review for that. What was more alarming to me was that things I had been successful at and normally got bonuses and praised for were marked down to good or average because *they were expectations for my job*. I felt like I was in the twilight zone and things I was being told could not be trusted. I felt like my boss was not supportive of me and at a time when I was most vulnerable.

I was emotionally bereft. I had always been a motivated and focused individual; now I felt like a fragile and small child. My career and professional status meant everything to me. I had been confident in my abilities and loved taking on challenges. My changing abilities stopped me in my tracks and I was looking at myself through a *disabled* filter. I had to acknowledge I had true weaknesses in my ability to perform my previous job roles. If I couldn't perform them, who was I? I felt like I knew myself, but now I wasn't sure who I was. I was so scared about my future. Everything from the dollars and cents perspective of supporting myself and contributing to my family to wondering how I could function in the world and social relationships. I had emphasized my ability to take care of myself and therefore to control what happened to me. Now I felt dizzy and like I was spinning out of control. Almost as though I had landed on a new planet and was unsure if or how I would survive. A mysterious and challenging journey was starting for my husband and me. I guess this was what an MS diagnosis meant when Paul and I were optimistic and hopeful when our marriage started. We had no idea that this would be the change that would happen to our family and me. An extremely challenging journey was starting for me. No one told me directly what I was failing at or what I needed to improve on and I felt insulted, insecure and like nobody cared about me. I had always poured an enormous amount of emotional energy into my work because I truly cared. I felt slapped in the face and that my caring wasn't reciprocated. I didn't ask for help because I'd never been in this situation and I didn't know how. Why didn't my boss, the employees, the people who knew me care about me? The events were just happening around me. I had been a boss myself for many years and I knew what a "problem employee" looked like. Now I felt like I was considered a "problem employee." I noticed my boss meeting with my staff directly and my meeting invitations declining. My boss got me interviews in different parts of the company because "she knew I was ready to move on to different challenges and I was "done" with HMO accounting." My fatigue with HMO Accounting was true and real and I was excited to interview and possibly move on, but when I interviewed in other areas of the Company for other positions, I was in over my head and unsuccessful. Most of the overall business was in areas I was completely unfamiliar with. After two different interviews with no job offers, I was discouraged. I started getting calls from a manager that was sort of in our area. She worked on different parts of the business and was running a system conversion team and needed help, "Would I be interested in joining her team?" I moved over to her team with another peer in the accounting group and I never was the HMO Accounting Manager again.

"An extremely challenging journey was starting for me. No one told me directly what I was failing at or what I needed to improve on and I felt insulted, insecure and like nobody cared about me."

My new role was very difficult for me to learn. I wasn't sure what a lot of tasks that I was supposed to be doing were. A lack of structure was not good for me! How did I end up as one of the people who were watchdogs overseeing the system conversion as it related to the accounting requirements for the whole company? The HMO Business that I was expert in was a carve-out from the main business, which was Stop-Loss Insurance. I was learning for the first time that the accounting I had been responsible for was merely for appearances' sake with each State's compliance departments. The legal entities I reported on had inter-company transactions with the parent company and ended up being eliminated in the consolidated company financial statements! So much for being a highly-regarded expert in the important area of HMO Accounting. The new position I had taken was deadly for me in many ways.

One day I went downstairs to eat lunch. It was a beautiful day and I chose to eat my lunch outside. I was looking around at the other people also eating their lunch and I thought I saw someone I recognized. I had to look twice to be sure, but I was right. I was looking at someone who I had worked with in the past at a different company than where I was now. I had worked with him when I was first out of college a long time ago. After tapping my courage, I managed to say hi and talk to him. He was working as a contractor for my company in a different building and a different department. I think we discussed my current job and some of my frustrations. Where he was working, there were some open positions and they needed help.

I got a call soon after that from the person in charge of interviewing for those positions and I started the interview process. It was a position that was created by the implementation of the Sarbanes-Oxley law. I thought I could do this because as a new auditor out of college we had to document processes. That was all this was.

I wasn't sure the position was right for me but it was a good position and it wasn't the horrible special project position where I struggled. I was hired to be a Sarbanes-Oxley Financial Analyst. I was now set-up for my next trauma.

I struggled to complete my work on time and within the deadlines. When I did complete it, and submit it for review, there were a lot of comments and corrections. I often had to go back and re-document and re-ask operations questions. I was completely out of my realm. I was now a poor performer in a place I'd never been. My coworkers who knew this work had to help me and work hands-on with me. I felt embarrassed and uncomfortable. Worst of all was the horror I experienced in my head because with all the explaining and extra supervision, I knew in my heart how much I just was unable to understand. Yes, they explained it well and I thought I understood, but if I was attempting to do it on my own I continued to make mistakes. I felt miserable and confused by the experience. For the first time in my life, I couldn't figure out what I needed to do, do it, and accomplish it. That had always been my approach to living life and I thought it would always come through for me.

I still saw my therapist Pat Daily on a much-reduced basis, and I talked to her about all of this. We had talked about cognitive problems with MS and I was always asking questions about what it meant. Resources for people with MS were sometimes available but hard to find. Pat referred me to a Speech Language Pathologist who could formally evaluate me. The problem with cognitive problems is they are invisible (mostly) and they're in your head, literally. I have wondered and worried about cognitive problems since I first read about them. I had read that the percentage of people with MS that have cognitive symptoms is high; most people have them. I knew I needed an objective and formalized evaluation.

I started on a path that was going to be arduous, painful, and filled with momentum. Once started there was no controlling the outcome. Historically, I've been a good test taker in general in my life. I knew I was seeing this specialist about my problems; the starting point in the process was with taking a test. While taking the test I was aware of some things I was doing which probably weren't right. I had to look at some backgammon-like game pieces on a small board in a certain order. There were pieces on certain triangles and omitted on others. There were different tiers and rows of pieces, one, two or three. She placed them on the board and asked me to remember how they were arranged on the board. I stared at them hard to memorize how they looked. I was sure I had it in my mind. Then she removed the pieces and handed them to me to place back on the board as they had been. This type of exercise is where I feel my deficits like black spots in my brain. I think, but there is nothing there to help me. I looked at it carefully and completely, but when required to remember the pattern I did my best but there were no keys to unlock the memory from my brain; it was like I had never seen it.

Another test was a logic test with a card with four squares; the first three were patterned; the first was on the top left of the page, the second on the top right, the third on the bottom left, the fourth on the bottom right. Rather than a pattern, the fourth square was blank. By looking at the changes in square one to square two to square three there was enough information to discern what the fourth pattern should be. Then there was a solution card with four patterns on it, and I was supposed to pick the square that I thought completed the pattern on the first page. The cards were arranged in a three-ring binder; the complete test consisted of flipping through problem after problem and solving them one at a time. At the end of the binder I was finished. I thought this type of test was easy with my DuMond brain. I felt gratified by her indication that I had performed well on that test.

I patted myself on the back. I clung to my 'intellect card' as a credential. However, by the end of the battery of tests and her results report, I felt ill. The test results showed a definite disability. I felt a mixture of relief in being validated that the problems I experienced on a day-to-day basis were not imaginary. Also, I felt the fear that MS was silently progressing and I wasn't the same person who I had been. I had been losing parts of myself even though I could still walk. The testing had shown that my specific cognitive issues were deficits related to short-term memory, attention to detail, multi-tasking and executive function, and word-finding (no more Scrabble). These were all skills that contributed to success in my profession. I could not succeed as CPA without these skills, particularly as a high-level manager. Apparently, my long-term memory was not impaired. I have the memories of my life and I have my long-term skills. I can drive a car and I can be successful with my area of expertise of HMO Accounting although even in this area I was carried by a staff that performed exceptionally well. I was no longer the accountant to be preparing the detailed journal entries or the statutory financial statements. At least now I also had the explanation and validation about why I struggled with the recent *new* jobs I had been doing. My ability to do *new learning* was and is what is now impaired. I can be taught something one day and not remember it the next day. I was working hard, but was not able to attain the success of mastery because of a lack of retention. As I reread earlier parts of this Chapter, I see my executive function disability play out in real time. From all the various struggles described here I can see how my ability to function was impaired. No wonder I felt so lost and hopeless at that time in my life!

My deficits cause problems in my non-work life, too. The need for multi-tasking skills appears everywhere in my daily life now. I'm a stay-at-home mom and homemaker. Listening to my husband and daughter's conversations, and interacting with them are the joys of my life. If I am responsible for preparing a meal and timing everything to serve together, those are two separate tasks. Being able to do them at the same time, something I would like to be able to do, can be a nightmare. I love my family and I love cooking. Preparing a quality meal for them and enjoying kitchen banter before we sit down and eat it is important to me. My husband will not come into the kitchen so that I can concentrate. He'll experience pain from his interpretation and perception that I'm not paying attention or not listening or not valuing what he is saying, though I am. I love our conversations; I love listening to him. If we had a cook and we sat around talking while we waited for the meal to come, I would truly value and enjoy each conversation.

Even my daughter can detect my cognitive problems.

At the age of about seven, my daughter would ask, "Why don't you remember?" or, "Why did you say sweatshirt if you meant pants?"

As she got older and into her teens, she now understands more how MS affects me. She understands some of my MS issues as they are happening and she has some angst about knowing I am affected by MS. No wonder at times, I have a hard time with friends. My long-term friends are usually patient with me. Then again, I've got to be irritating to be around frequently or for long amounts of time.

I went back to work knowing I would be filing for disability. It was a duplicitous experience. I went about my normal work-day as best I could with my normal struggles while I was re-searching the process of filing for disability from my company's disability insurance carrier. As best I could tell, I would have to indicate a disability date. Normally, a disability like a seri-ous injury from a car accident would happen and that would be the date. How would you establish a date for something like this? My MS started in August of 2000, my difficulties oc-curred over time but not overnight, and my testing was done in December. I decided to focus on work-related problems.

My husband and I talked about the variables and factors to consider. After we had decided, I picked a time to meet with my boss. At work, I had never told anyone I had MS, and it had been a taboo subject for me. I didn't want word to get out into my network and have there be a perception that I was incapable in my field. Now it was true. I told my boss I had MS, but I couldn't do it without starting to cry. I didn't want to cry because if I cried a little I probably wouldn't be able to hold back and I would cry a lot. He was quite shocked, and

I'm sure had no idea how to respond. I told him I would be leaving on disability. We talked about it and determined my last day of work would be March 1st. Therefore, my first day of disability was March 2nd: six short years from the date of my MS diagnosis. From the National Multiple Sclerosis Society's website, "cognitive dysfunction is one of the major causes of early departure from the workforce".

This date was a big milestone in my journey of loss, but it was only the first step. Once started, I was like a leaf floating on a river. I have felt buffeted around from one step to the next step without my having very much control over it. I applied for disability insurance. The company kept denying my claim. I had to get records from my doctor and submit it with the speech-language pathologist's report. I finally got approved for short-term disability and got paid 50% of what I used to make. If I had paid better attention or had some help at the beginning of the previous year, I could have elected to pay for a few pennies more for disability insurance to cover 100% of what I used to make. Then I had to file for long-term disability that eventually was approved. I thought the administrative bureaucracy was bad, but it was worse to feel unnerved and disorientated. Waking up each day without a job which was my very identity, made me feel invisible, unimportant, and purposeless. Considering a bleak future of the unknown as far as I could see was terrifying. My self-esteem was hard to come by. It didn't make logical sense. I had my husband and my daughter who were very important to me and I was important to them. But I would still need to find my new identity and re-define myself.

Chapter 8

DAILY COGNITIVE STRUGGLES

Oh Divine Master, grant that I may not
so much seek
To be consoled as to console,
To be understood, as to understand,
To be loved, as to love:
– Excerpted from Peace Prayer of St. Francis

As I mentioned earlier, some cognitive issues came to light in my work and eventually led to my going on disability. Here I would like to explore MS and cognitive issues a bit more deeply.

One of my hallmark abilities has always been multi-tasking. I also haven't been a list person. I felt largely confident in my ability to keep track of things in my head. It was amazing because I may have been putting myself in a pressure-cooker by my lack of organizing, but I really could remember and would think of the important item to be purchased at the grocery store or the important deadline coming up at work just in time to not miss anything important. It worked great for my career as a Certified Public Accountant (C.P.A.). Multi-tasking is a required skill because each day could bring a variety of tasks and meetings difficult to plan for. I also paid attention to detail, a skill required for managing accountants, publishing financial statements, and dealing with regulators and other members of a company management team. Couple this with an on the fly, disorganized personality, and I was a get it done on time and not a minute earlier person. I always predicted that after the busy season was over (mandatory 55-hour work weeks) or after completing and mailing an important financial statement filing, I would probably get sick with a nasty cold. I always did, and for a long time I thought that always happened to everyone. The continual adrenaline rush leading up to the deadline and the resultant pride I felt in myself when my team and I had completed it was my excuse for my exhausted immune system letting me down!

The purpose of this chapter is to examine MS and cognitive challenges. I'm particularly examining the type of person I was before MS and the way I live since my MS diagnosis. I had this career and did this type of work for sixteen years; six of them were after my first MS symptom and ultimate MS diagnosis. My last three years of work were during the three that I had been pursuing fertility treatment, getting pregnant, having my daughter eight weeks early, which was when my four-month maternity leave began, and visiting the NICU daily for the six weeks she was there. I was home with her for six weeks once she could come home. After that I was back at work, and she was either with her Dad or in a home day care setting. I never felt as though my work was my passion, but I did get a lot of out of it socially and financially. The last job I had seemed like it had fallen into my lap with a call from a recruiter when I had no job and was trying to make a go of it as a writer from home.

These days, when I make oatmeal for breakfast for Sierra and myself, I am proud of myself because I remembered to turn the hot burner off when the five-minute timer sounded. The frequent, scary, and annoying routine that has been occurring is that I will be eating or making my daughter's lunch and my husband says, "Are you done with this burner?" Then he turns it off for me. It is true that the burner is only on low since the oatmeal simmers for five minutes after turning the heat down. Before Paul was home with us regularly at breakfast time, it might be hours before I noticed I had left the burner on. Nonetheless, I did detect it. That's pretty bad, right? On the other hand, it's not like I set the house on fire. The scary reality of my cognition's deterioration is that I'm not sure what I experienced cognitively for this minor yet bad mistake is significantly different than what I might experience cognitively on a bigger scale and with a worse outcome. Thus, I wonder if making a small mistake would be the same cellular neurological process as it would be if there were a tragedy, a real accident, or an emergency.

I opened and read my email today and I had an urgent message that I had left my purse at my friend's house where I went to a gathering with other moms last night. Until I read the message, I hadn't realized it was missing. These are the types of things that happen to me daily now. Much of my time and energy is spent trying to analyze where I go wrong with my mistakes and what actions might mitigate the frequency or severity of the errors. I'm officially disabled and can be at home now with society's permission. However, it is hard to give myself permission and forgive myself for not being able to earn a living and help my husband with the financial responsibilities, like I used to.

The change in my work performance was probably more gradual than I remember. It seemed sudden, but I was seeing signs and, in hindsight, not putting them together until later.

I read or heard that MS could cause cognitive problems. I didn't understand what exactly cognition was even though I had heard the word.

The American Heritage Stedman's Medical Dictionary defines cognition this way: The mental faculty of **knowing**, which includes *perceiving, recognizing, conceiving, judging, reasoning* and *imagining*.

I would describe my mental deficits as problems with 1) attention, 2) short-term memory, and 3) executive functioning. I didn't know what the third one was except I was almost certain I needed it to be a C.P.A. I think you need it to be a housewife also. But the Stedman's definition is clear and to the point for me. Each aspect of knowing can look to other people like a character flaw instead of a disability. These are especially difficult for me even to be aware of and notice while I'm experiencing the problem(s). I am sad about not having access to these abilities the way I used to.

It turns out the percentage of people living with MS that experience problems with cognition is much higher than the medical community used to understand. I do not experience difficulties walking but I struggle with how to live with cognitive issues. One time I was driving an unfamiliar route. I'll never forget how surreal this experience was. I sat at a stoplight, waiting for the left-turn arrow. The light turned green and I proceeded to turn. As I was turning and after the turn

I couldn't figure out why something about the road looked odd to me. I drove for a fraction of a second, then noticed there were cars coming toward me on the same side of the road! I still didn't understand what was going on but largely by instinct, I waited and planned to pull my car to the right. Once I had done that, everything looked normal again. I think I continued to drive to my destination, but I had to revisit this in my thoughts before I finally understood what had happened and what mistake I had made. The road I turned left onto was kind of wide with a median in the center. I had turned left and gotten on the road *left* of the median, heading toward on-coming traffic. I was lucky because at that moment the oncoming traffic was very light. I had a decent amount of time to get from that side of the road and back to the correct side. Also, the median was small and not long, so I just had to cross the double-yellow line to be back on the correct side of the street. I'm sure there was at least one person driving the correct way on their side of the road that noticed what I had done, but it wasn't a narrow escape for them or me, thankfully.

Now, six years later, I have designed my life to keep my driving very local and usually not more than five miles at a time. The circle of my life is on a stage which is rather small. I drive Sierra to and from activities that are close to our home during the daytime. There are times I take longer drives than a simple errand, but I realize I need to put my attention and awareness hat on before proceeding. I'm going to try to describe something very hard to describe: there are times when I feel disconnected to my reality. You could say I've zoned out. I've just recently noticed that I experience this. I must notice when I'm experiencing this and consciously pull myself back and connect to reality. It is almost like a choice, but I must be able to detect when it is happening. That is the difficult non-choice part.

I'm in a clinical trial right now and taking a new drug. I attribute some of this new awareness to that drug. However, I am trying to measure something that is difficult to measure changes in cognitive ability using my memory to compare before and after to decide what changes have occurred. There are some actual measurable activities the study I'm in is quantifying. There are quantifiable improvements that the researchers can see although my cognitive deficit is not gone. I have an awareness and feeling that I need to make hay while the sun shines. I know I can't see my future with this disease, but I feel I need to write my story while I can remember it and while I am able to write it.

I miss my ability to reason and judge. The mistakes I make manifest themselves in missed appointments, double and unreasonable scheduling (I think it makes sense and we can reasonably have the time for all of them), and having difficulty planning my day because I think of something and then forget all about it. My husband and I have conversations when I make a mistake. We are always trying to unwind the issue, what the cause of the problem is, and how I can avoid making the mistake again. I think this is fine to a point and we can prevent many future errors. However, the mistakes are related to the detailed thought processes in my brain and I have little self-awareness or control over them. It is difficult if not impossible to change and improve my perception processes, since the part of my brain that processes perception has been damaged and is no longer working properly.

I feel badly when I struggle with memory or I do not know the right word or say the wrong word when I'm with my daughter. She can detect these problems. When I'm telling her to do something and I use the wrong word, it is confusing to her and not particularly effective parenting. If I forget something, it affects her and she later asks me, "Mommy, *why* didn't you come have lunch with me?" We have now told her and explained that I have MS and she sees how it can affect me.

Cognitive problems in MS are in large part not detectable to other people. What other people might see is something I'm doing that makes it look as though I don't care (sending cards on time) or that I'm not acting like someone else is important or valuable to me. It may happen when I have forgotten our last conversation or a person's name. It is not possible for other people to know how and when things are challenging for me in my thought processes or the extreme amount of effort it takes for me to prioritize and remember what I want to remember. Although I am sure that it is not true, I imagine that people would have an easier time understanding a physical disability because they can see it, though I'm positive that is absolutely not the perspective of someone who is in a wheel chair. However, all my symptoms can look like character flaws, and that is hard for people to deal with and understand. In the end, I feel isolated and I am frequently alone. That contributes to my feelings of being different and it is hard to put myself out there. Then I feel more alone. I recently missed an appointment two times in one week before I finally made it on time on the third try. The first time I had forgotten my wallet (insurance cards) and had to turn around

"I have an awareness and feeling that I need to make hay while the sun shines. I know I can't see my future with this disease, but I feel I need to write my story while I can remember it and while I am able to write it."

and go back home—and reschedule the appointment. The second time I arrived fifteen minutes late partly due to my lack of knowledge of where I was driving and getting lost. The third time the doctor ran late and in the end, I spent two and a half hours of my day for a fifteen-minute thyroid appointment. It is easier to live simply, stay home, and avoid the hard work. My cognitive disability is a daily battle for me.

Cognitive impairment is literally in your head. I am a person who lives in my head all the time. I think and analyze and have always been more focused on logic and places where I could get the right answer. That is how I chose and worked in Accounting. I had trained myself to become left brained. Any creativity or humor that came from my right brain effectively was squashed and pushed down as not having value.

Now the world looks different since the skills and tools I used to live in the left-brained world are not available to me anymore. I recognize now that the creative, right-brained way of living has so much value and is also necessary! I struggle with overseeing the household and the cleaning and organizing, although my mom was successful at it. I never valued it since it wasn't left-brained the way math is. Now I see there is such merit in being able to have these skills.

I rely on the Holy Spirit to be with me throughout the day.

There have been many times when I've been in situations where if I kept driving the way I was driving there might have been an accident. One time I was driving and turning right to merge onto a busy street. I turned and was sort of sloppy about how I merged. While I should have merged into traffic in the lane to the left of the merge ramp and had begun to do just that, for some unknown reason I felt a compelling need to turn the wheel to back to the right. I continued straight in the merge lane, then looked left at the car next to me, going full-speed. One glance into the terrified eyes of the older couple inside reflected the reality of my situation and how I had just avoided an accident though I would have been the cause of it! Admittedly, I was terrified along with them!

Amazing things seem to happen while I'm out in the world even while I make mistakes, and I stay protected. I am reminded all the time that Spirit is watching over me and making sure I'm here on the planet to be the best mother I can be for Sierra and the best wife to Paul. Now I've learned to call on the Holy Spirit when I'm traveling, driving, or doing something difficult because I know that the outcomes will always be better.

Chapter 9

HIGH-RISK PREGNANCY

May the Lord Bless you, Keep you, and Give you Peace
— Sign at Light of the World Church

Paul and I always wanted more than one child. After the miracle of Sierra's birth, I was calm and felt assured that I would have another child and maybe more because we had a successful IVF cycle. This meant success in getting pregnant with Sierra, but it also meant possible success if we wanted to have more children later. Therefore, we had good quality embryos (they had developed to a certain point, which made them more viable) available for the next time we wanted a child. For me this was an extremely big deal. Having gone through the questions and unknown times of not being sure I would be a Mommy and have a child, this level of success in the fertility battle was huge for me. I had wonderful potential children available to me without redoing the complete IVF protocol. A bonus in my mind was also that my embryos were frozen when I was age thirty-six. Thus, even as the years went by I thought I was in better shape than another woman my age to have a child. This topic and the specific details were on my mind continually.

After Sierra's birth, her newborn years were challenging for Paul and me. Maybe it is always that way, but I attributed a lot of my stress to her being born prematurely and being so small. It was clear I had post-traumatic stress disorder symptoms in the month following her birth. I struggled with depression, and the inherent lack of sleep you have with a newborn baby didn't help. I also struggled with breast-feeding. Sierra didn't learn to latch on well, and I pumped the milk that she drank. I always had enough to keep up with her, but I had to be on a rigid and strict schedule of pumping every three hours all 24 hours. I started pumping in the hospital right after Sierra was born. I lost sleep staying up throughout the night during the six weeks when Sierra was still in the NICU. Once she was home, I wasn't sleeping well in the 1-½ to 2-hour windows between caring for Sierra at night and keeping to the pumping schedule. There were times when Sierra cried that I couldn't get to her as quickly while I was pumping. That tore my heart out. I loved her more than anything. That is why I pumped and wanted her to have breast milk. It felt humanly impossible to be a good mother by this breast-feeding definition.

Things got better and easier as Sierra grew. Eventually she was sleeping through the night and it became easier and easier to take care of her. I knew I wanted a second baby this whole time. As my friends who had been pregnant when I was were having their second pregnancies and children, I knew I wasn't ready. Paul and I didn't discuss this much, but he wasn't ready then either. I loved taking care of Sierra and I couldn't imagine going back to the sleepless nights and the other first stages again.

Finally, when Sierra was four, I started to imagine having another baby. I started to think and dream about adding to our family. I had assumed for so long I would always have more children, and once I had made up my mind I didn't have any worries or anxiousness that there would be any problems. I started bringing up the subject with Paul, and I was surprised because he told me he was happy with our family the size that it was. I had to have more conversations with him to assure him that it would be okay because we had the great, healthy five-day embryos. I told him that I was feeling so much better now and that I would be different. I told him it wouldn't be as hard on him this time. I reminded him that even though I was now forty-one, the embryos were only thirty-six how great was that?! Finally, he conceded that I could call the fertility center and find out how we could start the process of doing a second embryo transplant and what all the other steps would be.

Then I was excited! I loved having the belief and understanding that I could be pregnant soon with Baby #2. Baby #2 was meaningful to me in so many ways. I wanted a second child because I knew my love for Sierra would expand exponentially to include the new baby also. I thought of all the stages of being a first-time mother during which I didn't know things, and I was so worried about whether I was doing it right or not. I built myself up by mentally looking at each thing about Sierra's birth that was difficult or that I felt guilty about and thought about how great I was going to do things the second time. I wouldn't be anxious about how I held the baby or if I was caring for the baby correctly with feeding, diapering, and playing with my future baby. Oh, and I was not going to have the same difficulty with breastfeeding either. I would be assertive and not let others tell me if and how I could breastfeed. If I had gotten to the same point where I had been with Sierra and it just wasn't working and I decided to stop pumping, I would have just stayed in bed with the baby and feed on demand so both my baby and me would be successful. I had been so critical and harsh toward my-self about everything about my experience when I had Sierra. Nothing was wrong about any of it, but I laid a heavy burden on myself for which the only response was to feel guilty and to beat myself up all the time. This future baby was a very special baby indeed! Through this second baby I would heal all my wounds surrounding the premature birth of my daughter. Also, I would heal the wounds of post-traumatic stress disorder and postpartum depression.

I started by calling the fertility clinic. We had to have some updated blood work before proceeding down the path of getting pregnant. We found out all the details of the cost of an embryo transfer which was expensive but not as expensive as the initial IVF procedure. I got a copy of the protocol I was to follow as prescribed by the doctor. I had reminded him that after Sierra's birth, a perinatologist I had seen had detected a protein S deficiency. That was the suspected cause of Sierra's slow growth and my severe eclampsia. The specialist had told me that I would need to have injections of Heparin to thin my blood and prevent clotting. With Sierra, I didn't use that drug, but then I got sick. For this baby, I was to start taking the blood thinner right away when my cycle started. So, I got the medications at the specialty pharmacy along with all the syringes and estrogen patches I would need. I felt like it was important to go to the same place I had gone when I was going through IVF and I became pregnant with Sierra. I did, but I was sort of disappointed that the staff working there weren't as excited for me as they had been the first time I was there, nor were they the same people.

Aside from the blood thinner, all the steps we needed to go through were pretty much the same. Certain injections of hormones at certain times, patches at certain times, regular blood draws to monitor my hormone levels. These were all complicated steps the first time I went through it. This time it was much easier, and I didn't have to call the nurse for questions as frequently. Finally, I was getting closer to the day when the embryos would be thawed and then inserted into my uterus. For the first time, I had internal mental chatter about how it doesn't always work. Like last time, though, I kept my thoughts positive and believed, "Of course, this is going to work. I always get pregnant the first time!"

The day of the transfer Paul and I went to the Center together. This stage in the process is very exciting! It was an amazing day when we did this to get pregnant with Sierra. One of the things we would find out for the first time was how our embryos looked. Earlier, we had decided with the doctor that we would thaw three of our frozen embryos. You don't know the quality of the embryos until they thaw, and if it isn't good, you don't have the time to choose another one to thaw. So, we went with three to ensure at least two good ones. We waited for our scheduled appointment time. When they called us back (me in a hospital gown) I couldn't wait anymore. First the doctor came in and he updated us on the thawed embryos. The quality of the embryos is given a letter grade (by what criteria, I don't know). Two of the embryos were A quality and one of them was B+ quality. Great news! The process to transfer the embryos was identical as before. I laid on an exam table and tipped back so that I was at an angle with my head lower than my legs. The doctor used a thin catheter that he put into my uterus which made an uncomfortable but brief pinch. The embryos were brought in on a special cart by the embryo team who were responsible for everything about our embryos. The doctor transferred the three embryos into the catheter tube. An imaging machine was to my right. The doctor could see my uterus and the catheter with a visual picture; which ensured the catheter was in the right place. I could see that and though I couldn't see the small embryos, I visualized three great embryos now nestling in my uterus. I had to stay tipped back slightly for a half an hour or so. Paul and I were in the room by ourselves, and we talked while we waited. The last time, with Sierra, we had followed most of the same procedures. The one thing that was new was that now I could see the embryos under a microscope in the petri dish since they show the image on the wall before the doctor transferred them! The last time only Paul could see them because he was standing and able to look. Finally, I could get up and get dressed. They encouraged me to recline in the car for the drive home, and I did this with my legs up. I could go about my normal routine after forty-eight hours of bed rest, but Paul had to be available to watch Sierra while I was resting, because she was just four. I had certain hormones I needed to continue taking and a blood draw schedule so the Center could monitor my hormone levels and adjust them accordingly. I also had a specific day scheduled for my pregnancy test, which was very exciting! You just should wait patiently for the time until that day before we would find out if it had worked. The day finally came for the pregnancy blood test, which was in the morning. We didn't get the results until around 4:00 p.m. It is a challenge to stay positive all day while you're waiting… Finally, around 4:00 the phone rang and the caller ID had the Center phone number on it. The call I awaited! I answered the phone, and it was my nurse who told me the test was positive and we were pregnant! At this point I'm saying to myself, I *knew* it would work. The next big date was two weeks later when we could have an ultrasound to see how many babies were inside me. My blood levels were high during the waiting period before my pregnancy test. It was possible I was going to have two or three babies! Paul and I both felt relieved when we learned I was pregnant with only one. We were wholeheartedly excited! We looked at the perfect baby on the ultrasound. I was starting to think about Sierra having a brother or sister and us being a family of four; what I wanted. The next ultrasound (they are given on a regular schedule) was an emotional appointment. This time when we looked at the pictures we could see our perfectly formed baby, but the nurse pointed out a darker colored area around the baby, which they said was blood. To my untrained eye this didn't look good to me. The area was between the baby and the uterine wall, where the umbilical cord was attached and the placenta will develop by twelve weeks. We talked with the nurse afterwards and she recommended I stay on bed rest and take it easy for the coming weekend. She said that frequently the problem resolves and the pregnancy goes to term. Just the way she talked about it made me notice the unexplained detail she didn't mention which is "What happens in the cases that don't go to term?" We changed our weekend plans of driving to Winter Park to visit my father while he was in Colorado. My Dad had a questioning tone in his voice when I explained why we couldn't come. I don't think he understood how serious I felt our appointment had been. He was expecting a Sierra story, but this story was different. I was newly pregnant. I still had blood tests and took hormones and the blood thinner. The doctors bumped up my dose of the blood thinner periodically. This period had been a relaxing fun time for me while I was pregnant with Sierra. This time was different. We decided to tell only our immediate family and to wait to tell friends. Something about this pregnancy was less certain than before.

The days after that passed uneventfully. I took Sierra to preschool and her other activities. She was a typical happy four-year-old. I went to appointments and got my blood draws as normal. Eventually, they were weaning me from the hormones I was taking so I could be off them by twelve weeks. I started seeing a perinatologist doctor at eight weeks. I was considered a high-risk pregnancy, and I wanted him involved with the pregnancy early. Then the day came when I came home and had a message from my nurse that my blood results were perfect and I could go off my hormones then because I was now twelve weeks pregnant! It was a bittersweet day for me. Paul and I had plans to take Sierra downtown for a concert, but right before we were supposed to leave

I went to the bathroom and saw that I was spotting blood. I was crying and upset and I felt like this was very bad. We ended up still going downtown but I was not happy at all. I found a place to stay seated, because I didn't want to walk around at all. Eventually we went home early. The bleeding had become heavier so I put on a pad. I called the doctor on call and talked with them. They were sorry to hear I was bleeding. I didn't like the sound of that. They told me to call back under certain circumstances, mainly surrounding how much I was bleeding. I filled up a pad. When I called back, I got advice to stop taking the blood thinner. I did for the weekend, but I didn't think anyone was telling me to go off it completely. I'm not sure if I didn't get good advice or if I just didn't understand what I should do. The details blur together after that. I know I had one emergency room visit to get an ultrasound to see if the baby was okay, which it was. I went to my doctor's office for an ultrasound and the baby was okay. Everyone treated me like a woman with a viable pregnancy since the baby was alive. I made another appointment sooner than normal at around fifteen weeks pregnant. The bleeding had lessened and wasn't bad like before at all, but it had never stopped completely. I continued taking the blood thinner as directed. I was adjusting, such as not lifting Sierra, avoiding carrying more than five pounds, and having Paul carry the laundry up and down the stairs. I tried to take it easy more, but I wasn't really on bed rest. We were planning a camping trip in our trailer to New Mexico where we were going to meet my cousins Mike and Becky. Paul did all the packing by himself. It was busy with Paul working, but we managed to have the meals planned and were all packed on Thursday evening. We were to meet them on Friday, but I had my doctor's appointment at 11:00 a.m. that day so we had told them we would be there late in the evening because we would leave after that. We left the house pulling our trailer to go to the doctor's office. It was a relief to have gotten out of the house ready for our trip because the preparations were not easy. I loved going to the doctor and being pregnant. I felt like I was in an elite group, I loved my doctor. I always felt good while pregnant, better than usual because of the hormones. We checked in and they took us back to the ultrasound room with four-year-old Sierra. The room was fancy and had a large screen to see the ultrasound on the ceiling. I was telling the nurse the status of my bleeding because I was feeling so hopeful about it as I was getting settled on the table. I noticed she wasn't responding to what I was saying. Then I noticed she was still moving the probe around on my abdomen. Finally, she said, "I'm not finding the heartbeat." My heart dropped. It was my worst fear throughout the whole IVF process. Hearing the heartbeat is the biggest deal ever: it means success, happiness and all things for the future. The biggest risk of not hearing it is early in the process and we had always heard it. In my mind, I kept thinking, "Keep looking, I'm sure you'll find it." Minutes were going by and she still hadn't found it. She said to me, "I'm so sorry. I'll go get the doctor." My mind was trying to understand and it wasn't. The scene couldn't be real and it couldn't be happening. My husband and I looked at each other in horror and disbelief. A part of me thought that the doctor would find the heartbeat. When he came in he was serious and he said hello and grabbed the ultrasound probe. After a moment he said,

"Oh, I'm so sorry, I was hoping we would get through this." I started crying. I was shutting down inside. He was talking and I couldn't hear him. Sierra was starting to notice something was happening and the nurse took her out of the room to get her some juice. I'm glad Paul was there; I needed him to help me understand what was happening. The doctor scanned my uterus and was showing us how the placenta had pulled away from the wall of the uterus. Even to us we could see the confusing ultrasound picture horribly and clearly. Just two-and-a-half weeks before, we were looking at the fully formed placenta which is large and complete by twelve weeks. I've always found it to be amazing. The doctor was saying that due to the size of the baby now, I could choose to have surgery or I could choose to deliver the baby. I had some lame conversation where I said, "I'll deliver. If I can avoid surgery, that is better, right?" Neither option was understandable to me because both were about solving the problem of having a baby inside me that was no longer living. He said if we delivered, we would have to go to Presbyterian/St. Luke's hospital on Saturday night and be there 24 to 48 hours. My brain kept thinking no we are leaving today and will be gone this weekend and I think I even said that. Paul was holding my hand and he was saying, "No, we're not going now." It was a living hell and he was taking care of me now. We left that appointment together as a family. I was empty and bereft. I felt like I'd been holding my child in my arms and that he had been ripped out of my arms. There was nothing but emptiness. I could barely hear Sierra asking Paul, "Why is Mommy crying?" as we drove home.

At home, we tried to call my cousins to let them know we weren't coming. We never got a hold of them but we left a voice mail. I don't remember much on Friday, but it was weird because of course with the hormones, I still felt pregnant. I still loved the child inside me. We were supposed to check in to the hospital on Saturday night around 8:00 p.m. First, we had to coordinate having someone watch Sierra for us. I called my sister-in-law and even though I could barely talk through my tears, I told her we had lost the baby; could she come down and pick up Sierra and watch her overnight while we were in the hospital. She lived an hour away but she and my brother were available, thankfully. They picked her up Saturday afternoon. Saturday was a long day for me. As a family, we went to the outdoor pool. Paul and Sierra went swimming. I just kept thinking about my baby still inside me.

Finally, we drove to the hospital. We had never been there and it was hard to find the right entrance to get to the maternity ward. I would be on the same floor where deliveries were happening, but they had a separate room for me. I could tell that I was in a segregated pregnancy loss area that the staff all knew about. I never saw people in labor or with their newborns or any people at all. The process started with a pill that they put in my vagina which would soften the cervix and start labor. Before I let them do it, I asked if they could do an ultrasound just to make sure there hadn't been a mistake. They were nice and did that, but as before, they could see the body of the baby, but there was no heartbeat. I cried throughout this process. They treated my pain to the level I wanted. With Sierra's birth, I was motivated to do the process naturally and without medication for her benefit. Now there was no extra credit for suffering in pain so I asked for an epidural after ibuprofen didn't work anymore. It was my first and only epidural. I slept some but I woke myself up dreaming and wailing one time. A deep motherly loss. It was instinctual and from my gut that I had to let that pain out. By early morning I felt something strange as if I was bleeding and I asked Paul to check what it was. We were supposed to call the nurse once the baby came. The baby had arrived and it was very small. It was strange that doctors and nurses didn't need to be there when it happened in this case, but they didn't. Once the nurse came back in she cut the umbilical cord so we could hold the baby. We didn't know the sex then (the baby was so small you couldn't tell by looking) but the doctor checked for us later and told us it was a boy! Sierra's baby brother! We decided to name him and the name I came up with was Matthew.

I had to wait until my placenta came. The nurse asked us if we wanted to hold the baby. We said yes and she gently laid him on a pillow and brought him over to us. He was so sweet and little. His body was red so he didn't look like a live baby. We wished we could know what color his eyes were and hair. We were curious if he and Sierra would have looked the same. Paul said of course they would, he said that the baby would have looked like a baby Sierra with blond hair and blue eyes. We don't know for sure, but I believe that. We could have the baby blessed and a chaplain came in and blessed him, putting his hand on Matthew's little head. The event was tragic, but the state of Grace in the room was large and strong. It seemed like he was meant to be here, like we were meant to have that time with him in the hospital. Sierra was meant to have a baby brother even if she would never know him alive.

Then the doctor came in and said that since the placenta wasn't coming they would need to remove it surgically.

I didn't miss the irony of this need for surgery when that is what I had tried to avoid. So, they had to take the baby so they could wheel me to the surgery room. They asked if we still wanted to be able to see him after I came back. I couldn't stand the thought of just saying good-bye now. So, they moved him onto his pillow bed and Paul and I went for me to get prepped. They asked if Paul wanted to come in the room; he did. They told us that he could come in later and they would tell him when they were ready. They wheeled me into the surgery room where they did more prep with me. The anesthesiologist and doctor came in to get started. I wanted Paul to be there now, and I had to ask them if he could come in yet. No one had remembered to tell him he could come in. The doctor told a nurse to get him and waited until he got there. Finally, he came in and everyone was ready. I could feel myself gradually lose consciousness.

I was in recovery for a short amount of time. The dose of medicine I had was less than for a real surgery and so I wasn't as out of it. Finally, we came back into the room. Now the baby laying on the pillow just looked sad and not as an amazing miracle anymore. Our time here was winding down and soon I would be getting dressed. The nurse asked me if I wanted pictures and she said they would make him look as good as possible with props. I'm sure I didn't even get what she was talking about, but I said yes. So, she took the baby to do that and I said good-bye then. It hurt again but it seemed right. She came back with the pictures and an oval blue felt memory box. I couldn't imagine what was in it but I was happy to have it. The pictures were on a disc so I didn't look at them until later. When I did look at them I was happy to have them. They had a picture of his head and others with his feet and hands. They had put a tiny teddy bear next to him in one and a rose in another one. It was nice that I had something to remember him by even though without it I would never forget this experience. I felt like we were so close to having been a family of four. When God or the Universe changes the plans, it can be devastating. I had a hard time.

My grieving process lasted a long time. Matthew was born in July 2008. I wore my grief like a badge of honor and gave myself permission to do so. The experience was incredibly real for me yet it was an unambiguous loss. Most people I know never knew I'd been pregnant. I received some, but very few sympathy cards. I couldn't share the experience with someone unless I shared the entire thing. It was very difficult to take Sierra back to school. The end of the prior year I was pregnant, now this year I was going back not pregnant. Preschool moms are always toting other kids or may be pregnant themselves. It was hard not to compare myself not a great idea. A comparison is always unfair because I could always see what other people had that I wanted, but I never knew the picture of what their whole life was like. What I needed to do was focus on what I do have. I have my family. My husband is great and my daughter is great. I didn't need to ask for anything else. Maybe this was the exact right sized family for me and us. It is challenging for me just to have one child. At least with one I can give Sierra and Paul my best. Of course, Sierra is the best.

Who knew when I planned my perfect life that getting married and having children (at least two, maybe three) would look so different. Just decide and get pregnant, right? For me,

I am so lucky I got pregnant twice. Get pregnant, start planning for that baby to be in my life, right? I had no idea what could happen in a high-risk pregnancy. I always chose not to hear the high-risk part. It could have been worse. I could have been grieving in his new freshly painted bedroom. We hadn't done that detailed planning yet even though we were expecting him. New life and every child is a miracle. I knew that and I never forget that. Creating life is a powerful process outside of what we can assess and analyze. I give that process over to God. I'm sad it isn't the way I want, but my life is not over because of it. I have a great family and a great life to live and to live fully. I am here for a purpose, and I'm not going to waste it anymore. Dwelling in my sadness only made it hard for me to hear the messages about what my true purpose is. Now I'm living my life and I am listening for guidance and direction and I'm acting to move in the ways God wants me to move.

Chapter 10

LOSING MY HERO

The best remedy for those who are afraid, lonely or unhappy
is to go outside, somewhere where they can be quiet,
alone with the heavens, nature and God.
Because only then does one feel that all is as it should be.
— Anne Frank

Fathers are often larger than life to their children. In my family, we held my father up high on a pedestal. What Dad thought or what Dad was going to say was the true measure of a good idea. If you could impress him, then you were on to something. I used this measuring stick on myself when I read books, studied in school, chose hobbies and interests, and eventually met and dated Paul who became my husband. I looked at my father as though he made the best choices all the time. I expected I could do that in my life too.

My childlike infatuation with my Dad faded once I was an adult. When I was no longer dependent on him I could see his mistakes; at least what were mistakes to me. His military career earned him great respect. He retired after 28 years as an officer and his work helped during the Cold War. Much of his work is still classified so our country owes him a debt of gratitude. When our family went to his retirement ceremony we were split and damaged. My Mom went to this event, stood by my father's side, socialized as an officer's wife all while knowing that she planned to separate and divorce him. His intellectual, non-emotional ways were perfect at work, but they had not been good for his marriage.

I got my first big bike with a banana seat, red handles and all the perks around the time I turned eight. My brother Dan and I would take our bikes to ride, and we were excited because we had just figured out that the road from school to our house was on a hill. That meant we could ride it almost all the way without pedaling or super-fast if we did pedal. We were doing this bike ride one afternoon and I was going particularly fast this day. I remember this like it was yesterday. We were riding on the sidewalk which was kind of narrow, and every so often there was a mailbox that tilted out toward the sidewalk from the left. I got to a section where to my surprise, the sidewalk suddenly seemed exceptionally narrow. I was going too fast to handle that. My memory in slow-motion has me riding downhill; I adjusted slightly for the mailbox, overcorrected, and down I went from my bike. It was that time of day when the sun was bright and in your eyes. I slowly sat up, started feeling pain in my shoulder and started crying. My head was aching and I was upset. I managed to stand up, left my bike, and walked the rest of the way home crying. My poor brother rode both of our bikes home. When I got home I caught my mom at a bad moment while she was in the kitchen, and she asked me what was wrong. I couldn't tell her I was in such pain. I went to my room to lie down, mad that she wasn't comforting me. What stood out for me was my Dad getting home from work and coming to see what was wrong. I told him where it hurt (my right shoulder), and he looked at it. I heard him go back to the kitchen and tell my mom, I think she broke her clavicle. He took me to the ER that night and yes, I had broken a bone. They put me in an ace bandage, and we came home. That first night was the worst, having to find a way to sleep that didn't hurt it. I was a stomach sleeper, and I had to sleep only on my back. I felt like my Dad had come to my rescue.

When I was nineteen, my boyfriend and I decided to live together. He was the first person I had fallen in love with, and we weren't very sophisticated about our choice but to us it seemed like living together was a perfectly normal thing to do. I'm sure my father was disappointed. I dropped out of college, giving up a scholarship *and* moved in with my boyfriend. I had some phone conversations with my Dad about this, but for most of it I pushed him away because "I'm an adult, I can make my choices." That arrangement didn't even last for a six-month lease. I was really in misery by then and my boyfriend and I mostly were avoiding each other. It was hard for me, but I finally called my Dad. I told him we were breaking up and asked if he could help me move out of the apartment. He only asked questions involving logistics of the move. We planned for him to help me while my boyfriend was gone. He came over at the agreed upon time with my brother Dan. The two of them took my few pieces of furniture and boxes and carried them to the family van and we went back home. I felt like he rescued me again. Even though I'm sure he was disappointed in me, he never hassled me. He just helped me. I was always grateful for that. My break-up was something I felt ashamed of but he supported me anyway.

I didn't always get along with my father when I got older. Emotionally, I wanted to connect to him, but outwardly, he wasn't very emotional. I constantly would feel I was seeking his approval. His neutral or non-response to me was crushing. As I grew up, I distanced myself from him emotionally as much as I could. I'd gotten burned too many times. I thought I'd come up with a great strategy to protect myself. I thought I had it all figured out. Time, however, told the real story. I still needed my Dad so much and still sought his approval. When I introduced Paul to him, I was watching for all the *good signs* from Dad. When I saw what I thought was approval, I cheered inwardly and patted myself on the back for my good choice (which it was). When we were trying to have Sierra, I kept him in the loop about all the details. I even wrote up a miracle story for him when we were successful getting pregnant, which I learned later he saved on his computer. Every visit we made to California had some drama to it because I was waiting for the unconditional love I always yearned for. I usually broke down crying about something related to him before, during, or after going to see him. My husband would try to keep my focus on our family and plan a great vacation for us. I always felt stress if our plans didn't match exactly everyone else's. I wanted the time with my father to be perfect every possible moment. Perfection was a silly goal. I should have enjoyed the time I did have to spend with him instead of worrying so much.

While I was very consumed with the medical side of my pregnancy with Matthew and putting my energy into having a healthy baby, I got some strange emails from my Dad's wife Adrianne. The news about my Dad was confusing, and I had a lot of conversations with my sister, which filled in the holes. She understood the situation more than I did. In June over Father's Day weekend my father was scheduled to take a trip to Africa with his wife and her family. While in the airport my father was "acting strange." People observed it but didn't know what to make of it. They went ahead and went through the check-in process, boarding the plane. Once they were airborne Adrianne saw behavior which worried her. It worried her so much she called the flight attendant and asked to have the plane turned around because she felt he needed medical care. They did turn the plane around and while I do not know and may never know the details, she had him seen at some of the best East Coast medical centers where Adrianne's daughter lived. The short story is the doctors diagnosed my father with a brain tumor believed to be a return of the malignant melanoma that had been removed from his ear fourteen years before. I got wind of the information, but I was so focused on my thoughts and positive thinking I felt I needed to do to save my pregnancy, I determined I had no attention to give to my father's situation. It sounded like he was in good hands with his wife. I had to detach from his situation at that time in my life.

When we learned about the lack of heartbeat and then the need to deliver our baby as soon as possible, I called my mom and my sister. Paul asked me if I had called my Dad yet. I told him, "I can't, I don't want to." However, he made me see that I should call him and tell him. I was so nervous and scared to tell him of my perceived 'failure.' He was so sad and understanding. He was consistent; as always, he didn't have the words to say to me. He told me, "I don't know what to say," repeatedly. I knew he didn't. He needed to use his emotions to do that and it was a skill he didn't have. Bad things like that had not happened to him. He was sorry and feeling helpless about the loss of the baby.

After I had delivered Matthew and had been home a week or so, I received a strange phone call. It was John who told me he was Adrianne's son. I knew Adrianne had four grown children, but I had never met them. The only time anybody in my family had met them was at their wedding, which I didn't attend. John said he wanted me to know the situation with my father. He had horrible news that the doctors had given him three to six months to live. I was horrified and wanted to turn back time so I could be with my father. My sister and I hurriedly made plans to take our families to California to visit. We went in early August. My Dad's hair looked whiter than I remembered, but otherwise he seemed okay. We spent time together talking. He had had brain surgery where they amazingly removed his tumor. He was proud of that and he showed me his scars. He logically and simply explained how when he had the melanoma removed from his ear, he had gotten fourteen more years. Now it was back and maybe he had five more years. Five more years? He only had three to six months! I was in a surreal world. Was it my job to remind him of the diagnosis I had heard? Did he not know? How do people with such a diagnosis typically deal with it? Is it even possible for someone to deal with it? What about people with a surgically removed brain tumor? I did not tell him anything differently or lecture him at all. What is a grown daughter supposed to do? Especially one who is visiting in her father's house where her stepmother was living. She had been the main caretaker of him thus far. I had no reason to think she was not taking care of him. I can't even imagine the horrible events that she had gone through so far. It's not an easy path for anyone, I imagined.

I spent time with my dad and could be there when the physical therapist came to see him. I was stunned because he put on his good, polite, entertaining manners with her. I couldn't see how she was helping him, other than talking with him. He had been falling in the night when he rose to go to the bathroom. He had a huge gash on one knee to prove it. His bedroom was upstairs and he was still navigating the stairs himself. The brain surgery itself was suspected to have weakened one side of his body, which is part of why he fell. He and the therapist didn't talk about it or work on compensating strategies for him to practice, and I was really worried about him. I can't imagine what a loss of dignity it was when falling became routine for him. It ended up getting worse, with even less dignity. A few times I caught him talking and not making sense. Then he would be normal again, so I could think I imagined it. Once my sister was there, she and I thought we would try to help him improve his walking, something the therapist wanted him to do. He had a walker which he didn't use in the house. He was happy to go on a walk with us, something he loved to do. He didn't bring the walker but we walked with one of us on each side holding his arm. He hung on to us, and seemed to be doing okay. We walked down the street where I had lived and played from fifth to eighth grade. We had the lofty idea we could walk from the house to the corner. Dad did well but was getting weaker. He told us we should turn around after walking about two house lengths. My Dad had large, strong hands. I loved holding his hand when I was a child because I would always feel safe and protected. Walking my father home when he was counting on us to help hold him up was sad and unnerving. I was forty-one, but I felt as scared about the changes in him as a child afraid of being alone.

Near the end of my family's visit we talked my father into taking us out to dinner. He took us to his favorite place where you order a bucket of seafood, like crabs, mussels, and shrimp, and they empty the buckets onto the whole table to grab and to eat. It was incredible with nine people around the table. I was proud of myself because I kept shelling my crab legs perfectly (not what I usually do). I kept showing them to my father who would nod his approval and smile. He took his walker to the restaurant and he needed it to walk there. I watched him pay the expensive bill on his credit card even though we were offering to pay our share. I am sad when I remember that outing now. Dad was not eating much because of his medications and how horrible he was regularly feeling then though he didn't say anything to us. He was proud and felt it was important for his role as a father and grandfather.

I was so sad when I was leaving and said good-bye to him. He was still acting like we would see him in September when he would be in Colorado for his Winter Park visit. I couldn't stop crying because I wasn't sure when the next time would be that I'd see him. Regardless, I doubted he would be going to his mountain condo again.

I started calling him regularly to talk once I was home. I'm glad I could do that. My sister had been calling him to talk since June and since I couldn't have done that because of my pregnancy I was glad I could do it now. It was nice to talk with him and hear his voice, but he was still not the talker I am.

Then came the horrible day I called to talk to him and he wasn't making any sense and I couldn't understand him. I was frightened and I ended up talking with Adrianne. She told me his oxygen levels were tending to be low and she had asked the nurse to come out and check on him. That turned out to be the last day I talked with him. The nurse had recommended he go to the hospital; the next news I got was news he'd been admitted to the hospital. I told my husband I felt like I needed to be out there. That is when I found out how easy and inexpensive it was to fly round-trip from Denver to John Wayne Airport, which was close to his house. Why didn't I visit more regularly?

In the airport in Denver I bought a novel. On the plane, I read and visualized myself sitting by the bedside reading to him. I was planning to stay at the house and I had called Adrianne. Her son John picked me up at the airport and took me straight to the hospital. When I got there, Adrianne's daughter Gwen, who I had met before, greeted me. She wanted to help set my expectations and warn me that Dad would look not like himself. I prepared myself, or so I thought. He was in the ICU. I went into his room and he was in bed with tubes going into his mouth. He was on a ventilator and a machine was breathing for him. They had him very sedated so his eyes were closed. He looked much older than I remembered him looking only three weeks before. I had to accept that my vision of reading to him was not real. He was struggling to live. His hair was white all over, and his long body was in a hospital gown and his feet were bare. He was a tall man—the normal sized bed was too short for him. I spent that first day by his side. I saw Adrianne who was there while working on her knitting, but it was hard for her to be sitting there as much as I was. I talked with lots of doctors and asked the nurse about everything that was going on, what the numbers on the machine meant until my brain could somehow feel like it was under control and that there was hope. They were treating Dad with IV antibiotics believing he had pneumonia. They had taken a biopsy from his lungs and were culturing it. It would take a few days to know what exactly they were dealing with. I called both of my brothers and my sister. I recommended they come out. It was hard to be there alone without them and I felt a huge responsibility towards them. There were moments when Dad was off his sedation meds and could open his eyes. That was hard because he looked surprised and scared. He wanted to talk but couldn't. I held his hand and talked to him. I got a pad of paper and a pen and tried to help him write what he was trying to say. His hand was never able to hold the pen to write though he tried. The nurse showed me how I could swab the inside of his mouth with water to ease his dry mouth. He let me do this and it seemed to help him. One by one all my siblings came to see him and it was hard to see their shocked reactions. I made some other phone calls because I wanted to reach out to Dad's sisters and brother. I knew they were getting emails from Adrianne, but I know for me, I always wanted to know more. I had my cousin Becky's number in my phone so I called and reached her. Then she reached out to my aunts and uncle. I was using Dad's car while I was there. I would drive to and from the hospital and pick up my siblings from the airport and transport them. It worked out well and I became a semi-veteran expert of driving I-405, which was a wide freeway in southern California; the biggest I had ever driven. My brothers helped with the driving, which gave me a much-appreciated break. One by one my siblings had to return home. Toward the end of my two weeks I knew I'd be by myself again. My cousins Mike and Becky had come through for us. Mike drove out to Orange County from New Mexico to help his parents who made a trip out to see Dad. I was leaving early on a Friday and Mike came by the house and dropped me off at the airport. Again, I cried leaving my Dad but I so wanted to be with my family who had been without me for two weeks. I had planned future dates to come back but I needed to return home for Sierra and Paul. Once we had all left we had to rely on Adrianne communicating with us.

Denise and Don ended up coming back earlier than me. Then they were updating me. Once when they were updating me, there was a horrible phone call where Denise told me I had to come back. They had a specific date when they would take Dad off the ventilator. The doctors had always told us that the longest they could ventilate a patient was three weeks, then they would perform a tracheotomy, a hole in Dad's neck to use for the tube. That might seem like a simple dilemma and just about cosmetics, which is what I had always thought. In my mind, Dad was always going to be coming off the ventilator and yes, I knew he still had cancer to deal with but I hadn't started letting him go yet. He was from a family of near 100-year-old relatives. He had just turned seventy that March. I believed I had a lot of time with him in my future. This call was devastating. Dad had gotten worse since I'd been there. All the baby steps they had done to reduce his dependence on the ventilator had failed. They believed it was the brain injuries that were making him unable to breath on his own. The decision to do a tracheotomy was a question of whether you agree that your loved one should stay on the ventilator through their neck and move to a less costly facility where they would be kept alive as a vegetable. The doctors were now saying they thought he had bleeding on the brain and would never be able to come off the ventilator. Adrianne was the person Dad had designated to make medical decisions for him. It was a difficult decision for her to decide that he would not get the tracheotomy, to remove the ventilation equipment and it would just be a short time until he died. I immediately made plans to fly back. The date and time of September 7th at 1:00 p.m. was the time he would be taken off the ventilator. Returning was horrible and I was mainly supporting my siblings by being there. The day we went to the hospital and Adrianne signed the paperwork asking that he be taken off the machine was very dark and sad. The doctors asked us, his children, if we understood the medical decision, and we said we did. Dad's son Don and his two daughters were at his bedside along with certain adults and teenagers from Adrianne's family. Her older grandchildren considered him to be their Grandpa. No one knew what to expect after the tube had been removed. He could have lived for minutes or longer based on what the doctors had said. There were a lot of tears and a lot of praying for him, holding hands with him, and grief for the whole thing. After a few hours, the hospital staff tried not to be intrusive, but, they needed his ICU bed for the next patient. Dad looked as comfortable as if he was napping on the couch on a Saturday. With his children following along, the hospital took him from his bed to an ambulance. Then they moved him to an oncology facility on the same campus as the hospital. We could walk there and take our vigil to his new room. The room he was in was a welcome relief from the dreary ICU, with a window and no machines. The nurses came by in four-hour intervals to take his basic vital signs. They continued to be strong for the whole day. My father was going to do this on his schedule, not what someone planned for him. We talked with each other, joked with each other like kids, and prayed a lot. It was an honor for us to stay with him and a relief to see him in a much more comfortable setting. At around 9:00 p.m. Adrianne came in to take up the vigil from us. It was extremely hard for us to leave, but I had a strong feeling that he did not want to die in front of his children. At home, we went to bed with reluctance to semi-sleep and to wait for the bad news. My sister and I slept together in my old room at Dad's house and Don slept in his childhood bunk bed. The stark ring of the telephone woke me from a deep sleep. I struggled to get up even though I wasn't going to be able to fall back to sleep that morning. My sister got up, answered the phone, and from her comments I knew he had died. Adrianne had woken up early around 5:00 a.m. and he died with her in the room soon after. She always said he waited for her to wake up. Thus, on September 8, 2008 at the age of 70, my father David Lloyd DuMond's spirit left his body. It still brings me to tears. I then felt like a child all alone in the world even though

I'd been living on my own for eighteen years. I think the loss of a parent shakes up your security deep inside your body.

Soon after, Don had a flight to go back home and we said good-bye to him. Denise and I didn't want to stay very long in his house, but we had longer until our return trips. We decided to take the car to Monterey where our grandma, aunts, and cousins lived. Denise took us on the open road and did the driving. It was a freeing experience to be away from our sad hospital routine even though we were struggling with our loss. It was good for us to be in a safe place where we could be cared for, which we needed. Our Aunt Pam helped us get appropriate outfits for the funeral, which Adrianne was waiting to schedule at a The Riverside National Cemetery in Riverside, California. I had said I would do one of three eulogies for the funeral. There would be one from Adrianne's family, one from a military peer, and one from his first family, mine. I worked on it from my father's Macintosh laptop that he had loved and toted with him all around the world when he traveled and used for journaling. We stayed in Monterey in some denial. Paul and Sierra arranged to fly out for the funeral. Afterwards, we would all fly back to Denver together. Paul could not have been more supportive during this time. I ended up spending a couple of weeks in California and Paul covered all of Sierra's care when she was four years old.

* * *

The day of the funeral arrived. It was to be a military funeral with a memorial service, folding and presenting of the flag and full honors with a 21-gun rifle salute and bugler, with the burial to occur later. It was hard for me, as I knew it would be.

When we arrived, they had a tent set up for the memorial service. There was a photo of Dad from years earlier. It shocked and saddened me to see his face unexpectedly, but then I kept looking at it which was comforting. When I had been home, I managed to arrange for my son Matthew's cremation. Paul brought the cremains with him when he flew out. I had asked Adrianne if I could bury them with Dad since we hadn't had a service for Matthew at home. She agreed which made me happy, and she coordinated it even though it was very unofficial since we were bending the rules. So, at the memorial, my father and Matthew's cremains were in a decorative box. At the service, my sister and her family, my brother Don, all my Dad's siblings and my cousins Mike and Becky joined me. The beginning of the ceremony was for Dad, then they had the 21-gun salute. Then, a small group of family members had a small service honoring Matthew. I so needed that ceremonial part of my grieving. It was nice to be able to include my extended family in the loss of our son. After that there was a reception for a broader audience who wanted to pay their respects to my father at Adrianne's church. I was nervous for the eulogy and proud to be there and represent my family. The eulogies were wonderful because they showed how my father had lived his life and the reception afterwards was a celebration of all that he was. My brother Don was there in a suit and he looked and acted just like my father. He took his role as a representative of our family seriously. We all did and it was great to hear all the people there talk about their relationships with Dad. Soon it was over and time to move back to his house. All his siblings were there with us and it was great to talk to everybody who loved him as we did. We were all leaving the next day. It was sorrowful for me on the plane again, but I was so happy to be with my family to start the new chapter of my life that was beginning without my father's physical presence. I felt and knew I would always feel his spiritual presence within me in my heart.

Chapter 11

Personal Development and Growth

For I know the Plans I have for you, declares the Lord,
Plans to prosper and not to harm you.
Plans to give you a Future full of Hope
— Jeremiah 29:11

One of the coping strategies which helped me begin to live again, after enduring everything I've written about thus far, was travelling as a couple with Paul to attend business and personal development seminars. We went to an experiential outdoor camp together and experienced amazing moments at the outdoor camp seminars, sharing what we were learning with each other and what we wanted to do with that learning. I felt like the luckiest woman in the whole world. My mother had always wanted a more in-depth relationship with my father, and here I was at this place of growth with my husband. He not only started this process of development first and brought me with him but now we were sharing and talking about what was going on for each of us. I felt so blessed and so in love with my husband. This growth we went through saved me from the depths of despair I had been living in. Plus, it is giving us both a path to living a life of joy and abundance together.

One of our courses taught us about being a Wizard. What is that? It is as you might imagine a place of focus to create the life we want. I read the book *The Secret* years ago as my first exposure to a similar concept. In 2007, I did not have the skills to understand fully what the concepts in the book were. It almost seemed as if you just wished hard enough your heart's desires would come true. Now I see it a bit differently. I think it is critical to have a detailed vision of what you hold near and dear to your heart. The action was the piece that was missing for me in 2007. The Universe will move to create and manifest and support me in achieving my vision, but the momentum starts with me and my actions. I am creating this book with grace and ease. I still must set the time aside to write it. I make the commitment. I set the time aside. When I set the time aside, and I try to do what I commit to doing, then the momentum begins. When I sleep in and decide I don't have the energy to get up, nothing happens. When I sit at my computer and read email and surf the internet, nothing happens. When I follow my roadmap and stare at my chapter titles, inspiration moves within me. A blank piece of paper in front of me is a commitment. A thought process begun but not completed is a commitment; a thought process completed is creation, imagination and art. All these things are actions which move me forward and are a birthing and creation process. It is so much more beyond wishing and desiring.

My husband and I took self-development courses together over the course of one year. It was a great experience, and we both learned so much. A pair of courses we took were called Warrior Camp and Wizard Camp. Warrior Camp taught us we could quiet our minds and achieve our goals. Wizard Camp taught us how to think in a way that truly served us in the process of achieving goals.

One of the biggest lessons I learned during these courses my husband and I took is that my intellectual mind can be an obstacle. When I stick to the facts and only do the analysis I am cutting off all other possibilities. I thought facts and logic were all I could trust in and believe. I wrote this short letter to myself at the end of Wizard Camp:

"The power of thoughts and intentions truly change how my life is. Because of this, I'm a Wizard. I will create space and allow meaningful connections with people who are also Wizards. Be okay with where you are and live joyfully."

The energy of imagination and optimism are a hugely important ingredient to solving any problem. My beliefs about what things mean are completely responsible for the results I'm having in my life. What I had learned was that I had the choice of what to believe. I could believe that bad things were happening to me in the stories throughout this book. Otherwise, I could believe that all things happening to me support me. Because of the grief work I've done I can believe this now and in fact it seems completely obvious to me in some ways. I had the blessing of MS and learning the value of living my full life today. I am fortunate with my lack of mobility issues, even though I do have disabilities to deal with that are not visible. How many healthy people get physically

"The Universe will move to create and manifest and support me in achieving my vision, but the momentum starts with me and my actions."

trapped in their jobs and careers? Needing to stay where they are for achievement and recognition is a factor that keeps people from living their dreams. I had tried a sabbatical to stay home and write and it was difficult for me. When I had no choice and I had to find my dreams and mission outside of my CPA life because MS limited my abilities, I gained freedom from my self-imposed boundaries. I had a grieving process to go through, but I also had a gift.

It's interesting asking questions about why was I born into this situation and not another. Anyone born in the U.S. has it so much better than in other poorer parts of the world. Wayne Dyer says in his book, *Inspiration – the Ultimate Calling*, that we sit down with God and discuss and agree on the course of our lives, our challenges, and ultimately what our true purpose is. I don't have a single answer, but it is a good question for us to ask ourselves. I believe that my challenges are leading me to my purpose in my life. God still wants me to be here and I am still here, so there is no doubt that I'm meant to be fulfilling my purpose or purposes. When I think of it this way I start asking myself what's next instead of "Why Me?"

Wayne Dyer says that we all meet with Source before we are conceived and come to an agreement on who we are, what our purpose is, and who our parents who will help us best serve our purpose will be. I think about this scenario a lot in my life and then in my daughter's. Were my parents and my circumstances lined up to give me the life I've had, which is leading to me fulfilling my purpose? Did Sierra agree with Source that she would be an only child, with parents like Paul and me, and that she would be prepared to fulfill her purpose? I get more peace and comfort from this idea than I can find elsewhere. Nothing is an accident. Things don't always turn out the way we would have planned them.

What if I keep my questions framed around the idea that my specific challenges are there just for me, too and that they are to help mold and change me in some way? I used to get angry when people would say, "things happen for a reason" because I didn't think there could be a sound reason for any of the trauma and pain in my life or things that had gone wrong for me. I've learned to look at my life more like a wisely planned journey from God's perspective. I know I've grown and improved. I know I'm stubborn. The subtle hints I was receiving from the Universe about transitioning from my logical accounting life to a more creative and artistic one did not seem to be working and I largely ignored them due to fear. When you ignore subtle hints long enough, be prepared for the Universe to step it up and be clearer. The Universe gave me a solid shove out of my way of thinking when I received my MS diagnosis. Now many years later I see it as such a gift in so many ways because I have official permission to change my focus to my family life and to explore other parts of myself. Now I can see this problem with gratitude and as a blessing. I am excited about looking forward to and wondering what is next in my life.

Chapter 12

GRACE AND THE UNIVERSE

*See God in every person, place, and thing,
and all will be well in your world.*
— Louise Hay

The intention of this chapter is to speak of Grace and how it has been present for me throughout my life. Awareness of Grace is something you may learn about in church as the presence of God, but has also been for me, a coping skill. When I'm aware of God being beside me and with me throughout the day, I am comforted and confident. What is Grace anyway? I think of it as the Grace of God or divine assistance. I've experienced this Grace in small experiences (like getting the perfect parking space) and during horrifying and traumatic experiences. The strongest time was after the birth of my stillborn son. I was in agony about losing that child but there was a strong sense of spirit with me in the room. I believed that Jesus was there for me to lean into and he knew how I felt. I also knew that blessing the baby was important and recognized. I was grateful for Matthew and the experience even though it was awful. I wish I could have bottled up what I experienced and keep it on hand, because I felt grief in the hospital room but I could handle it. When I was in pain taking Sierra to preschool, and I had to tell people about our loss, I needed that same strength. However, in the real world, when I took Sierra to school, it was hard to be centered and feel the presence of God even though I knew he was there.

I feel like Spirit is with me in the real world by the small miracles that happen.

"Everything happens for a reason." People would say that to me after I lost Matthew. Sometimes, I also heard that mantra after I found out about having MS. I lashed back against that. There is no way to take such horrible life events and say the Universe meant for them to happen. What kind of a God would be so cold to one of his children?

It is crazy, because finally after all these years, when going back and seeing everything in hindsight, I can understand that maybe everything *did* happen for a reason. I put everything into my career. It made sense, I liked it, it was a good place to be. Nevertheless, there were terrible things about it for me. It was stressful and difficult and required a level of precision from me that I thrived on at one time, but over the years those things were unyielding for me. I woke up in the middle of the night with anxiety and fear about having made horrible, non-reversible mistakes; then I stayed awake the rest of the night. I never stopped feeling as though I would get found out, that I wasn't as good as I was made out to be. I had bosses that could make me doubt myself and feel distrustful. I had only one boss who made it okay to leave work on Friday without having completed every task. After all, there was always Monday to work on the current problem. Few people modeled a balanced life, and I struggled with balance in mine. In hindsight, I'm very glad to be out of the pressure cooker. I have a blank canvas upon which to create the life I want.

I always wanted a bigger family, but I have a small one. As much as it pains me to say this, my husband and I have the exact right-sized family. I hate thinking of MS taking away the future that I haven't had yet. The limitations I feel with handling everything in my home and life remind me that with MS I have a life, though I can't do anything and everything that I want. If we had a second child it would probably break all that we have. Paul is covering for me in ways I don't even really see. Therefore, he has an enormous amount of the responsibility. He did so much to help with Sierra as a baby and of course he is still helping at each stage. I'm not sure that he would have had the wherewithal to raise Matthew with me. I'm not sure that I would have had it either. This topic is the most upsetting to me. I can hardly stand the disappointment of not being able to have everything that I want. Especially when it seems like everyone else can and do have everything they want. I had two brothers and one sister; that is my normal. Sierra doesn't, which is her normal. I have no doubts she will be okay and maybe even better because she is an only child. But I know that sometimes she is lonely, and I just want to be able to improve that for her.

So, my planned life was not the plan the Universe supported. If everything was happening for a reason, the missing piece for me was knowing that those reasons were to serve me. Changes happened to me that wouldn't have been able to happen if I was on the same train tracks I had laid out for myself. I couldn't get off them or even see the possibilities. The big picture God has planned for me is bigger than I can plan and bigger than I can understand. I am being taken care of. I am not walking this journey alone. I have Jesus with me every step of the way. In the most difficult of times I do feel like Jesus carried me during the awful parts. I am here for a reason. I thought I could be the planner and that I knew all the reasons why I was here. God is showing me glimpses and hints that I should head in different directions, which sheds a whole new light on living according to God's will. My life isn't for me, it is for others and especially God. Everything about this concept is uncomfortable for me. Like it or not, struggling to accept it or living with grace and ease, this is where I am. I can only go from where I am. I can only live in the present moment. The past is over, and living there keeps me from living here and now in this moment. The future is unknown. I thought my system of doing things was protecting me. While I was working as an auditor and planning and attempting to prevent any bad thing that could happen, I couldn't live right now in the present. All the planning I did was a faulty way of protecting myself. The things that have happened to me are way beyond the scope of anything I could have prevented or prepared for. Since my worry couldn't stop them or prevent them from happening, I realize I could have at least been present and happier in the life I have. We all are dealt a hand from the same set of cards. Life is living presently and gratefully with what you have. Not just surviving, which I was an expert at, but also thriving and living with joy.

Personal development at forty-three: who knew I'd be doing that? I was a self-help book fanatic back when I was younger. I felt like I learned and changed a lot based on the information I learned from reading books. I put much of it into action as a skill. I had thought that by 'fixing it,' something in myself would also be healed. A lot of what I researched and learned early on in my adult life related to the dynamics of my family. John Bradshaw used to have a show on PBS where he used a very artistic and enormous mobile to represent how each person in the family is an object on the mobile and that the actions of one person unmistakably changed the balance of the mobile. I watched those shows as a young adult searching for answers about how my family of origin and I related to each other. Ultimately, by studying, I felt that I had learned the information, I was incorporating it into my life, and therefore, I was free to move on and become the free person I was meant to be.

That was partially true, and I'm sure a lot of the advancement in my career came about because of some of those learnings. In general, I was happy even though anything to do with my parents could knock me seriously off balance. A brief phone call, an in-person visit, or sharing a meal could activate old behaviors, patterns, and emotions. Hence, I started incorporating a safe distance from my parents. The less I needed my family the better off I thought I was. Seems logical, right? Package it up neatly with a bow, set it aside, and move forward independently. This method seemed like I was advancing myself at the time, but it did nothing for me when my father was dying. I coped with fear of abandonment by and fear of rejection from him by separating from him as an adult. That 'skill' was agony when all I wished for was more time with him and it seemed like time was short and I wasted the time I had with him.

I release things to Spirit. For me this is giving up control of what happens in each situation. While I'm living in this way I can feel the grace that surrounds me. I feel secure and relaxed. I end up meeting people randomly and notice that I am meeting just the right people that can help me at just the right time for me. I can break through old fears and behaviors while I'm in this place. I can expand my perspective and see things in positive ways. In the past, I felt left out and separate from other moms at my daughter's school. This year when I started feeling those types of feelings I focused on asking myself, "What kind of mom do I want to be?" Scared, nervous, and acting like I didn't need or want any friends? Or smiling and friendly and noticing other moms who are alone and not talking to anyone? This attitude has changed my experience of dropping off and picking Sierra up at school. I've met more moms, I've talked to moms I know who I don't normally talk to, and I've hung out to chat with more people than normal. I've let Sierra play on the playground for a while before we leave, too. I'm not experiencing those old feelings, because I'm different. I can't control others and how they act, but I can control myself and how I act! The way other people act is just a mirror of me and how I act in the world. If I want a different world I need to look at myself. If I change myself, the world that I see will change. Neat, huh?

The Universe surrounds our planet and even more. The Universe wants to create balance and respond to our needs. The clearer and more focused our imaginings are the easier it is for the Universe to provide them. The Universe arranged all the support I had through the journeys in my life and the pages of this book. I was mad and felt lonely when I wanted something like good health but then I found out I had MS. I felt like the Universe wasn't supporting me. In fact, here's how it went for me:

From symptom to diagnosis was three weeks. Many people with MS struggle with their health for years before a doctor finally diagnoses them.

The CHAMPPS study results were released not long before I had a conversation with a doctor about medication. Now he could make a recommendation to start on therapy right away and he didn't tell me we had to WAIT for a second symptom.

The area I live in has excellent doctors who are top in their field.

I was now living in the moment. I struggled to live in the present because I was so busy with many activities. I became hyper-aware of the present moment. I appreciated the current health of my body, the function in my legs, and my ability to see. I began to focus on what Paul and I were so blessed to be able to do. Here are two examples from my life, but I can see it everywhere now that I'm looking. We enjoyed visiting spectacular manmade destinations such as Mount Rushmore. We also enjoyed visiting as many of the natural sights as we could: hikes in Rocky Mountain National Park where we saw awesome plant life, mountains and animals in the wild like moose, elk and many others.

When I had to stop working and became disabled, lost my baby, and lost my father, I can see that the Lord supported me and walked with me in all those events as much as I hated that they happened to me. Everything happens for a reason even if I can't see the reason. Often the reasons can only be seen in hindsight and with enough time away from the event or events. God is the only one who can see the entire picture.

My vision and brain are limited to what I can understand. God is managing my little slice of life but also how mine relates to many other lives. That is daunting when I think about it. I'm glad I am not in charge of it all like God is. With my cognitive problems that would be bad for everyone!

I'm blessed to be in the place that I am. Through all my traumas I became more and more isolated. I felt alone without any support. Now I see that if I had changed my perspective slightly, I would have seen more options for support around me. If I expected to be isolated, I was indeed going to be isolated. I found a Yahoo support group weeks and months after I had Sierra—because of HELLP Syndrome. Each person in the group had had a similar experience as mine. I wish I had that support in the days right after I had delivered her to help ease the postpartum depression I suffered. But eventually I did find the group support I sought. After I had lost my baby, I found a support group for parents who had lost a child before birth. Again, I didn't have that support in the days after my baby's heartbeat was not heard, but eventually I did have support. It is such a relief to be with people that speak the same language and no translation was necessary.

My MS Support group serves the same purpose. We meet once a month. Everyone in the room is unique in their experiences, but we all can understand each other. There is always hope and joy in that room. I've learned from others and had wisdom available to me. I could share all my stories, and this group supported me through all the events covered in this book. The people there were a constant throughout turbulent times in my MS journey. Now, with my child being at an active age, I often can't make Saturday meetings. I am busy doing things with my family. In the worst times, I didn't even know how happy I would be only eight years later. It is amazing to realize that I couldn't see the path to healing, but I've now come out the other side. That movement and manifestation are the power of Grace and the Universe.

I even meet people with similar stories in the places I would never expect. I meet them and hear their stories and understand in my core that I am not the only one who has walked this path. Meeting these people helps clarify my vision. I have had this incredible journey and I'm alive and growing in awareness every day. I used to think my purpose was to have an incredible professional business career. Then the Universe soundly told me no. Later, I thought my purpose was to have a houseful of children. Again, I was told no. My MS, though, has stayed mild enough for me to continue to write and plan. My family relationships have continued to grow and to flourish. I now see a vision of women everywhere having a haven for support as it relates to their specific situation. For me, this would have been groups or counseling to help cope with infertility, MS, and loss of my parent and loss of my son. I would customize specific support systems for others. My idea is to create Centers for Women with Loss which would have different resources for obtaining information and connecting with others to build support networks for the difficult issues that no one talks about. These are the issues that isolate people and make them feel alone. I would love to be the resource that women like you could connect with for hope and support. I feel like this now is my purpose.

Chapter 13

BEING CALLED TO A RELATIONSHIP WITH JESUS

God grant me the serenity
To accept the things I cannot change:
Courage to change the things I can:
And wisdom to know the difference.
— Reinhold Niebuhr

I've always believed in God. I have childhood memories of asking my mom questions about what God looked like. I always imagined him to be a gruff looking character wearing '70s style dark glasses. He wasn't mean; he was nice and caring. I was raised Catholic by a very devout mother who went out of her way to not give us the hang-ups about God she had experienced when she was growing up and attending Catholic High School. I was never afraid of burning in hell. I figured God could deal with me and any problems, and those could be worked out.

I grew up, had my confirmation, and generally was okay with going to church, although I was a normal teenager and got bored with a lot of it. My Aunt Diana was my Godmother and she took her job seriously. I just thought she loved me and I had a good relationship with her. She was at my confirmation, meaning a trip to England for her! She spoke up when Paul and I had planned our wedding to be outdoors and not in the church. She wasn't at all harsh, but she got through to me enough for me to contact my church and discuss the whole issue. I worked with a great Deacon, and we arranged to come into the church the day after our civil marriage and have our marriage blessed by the church. Because I had my Godmother to talk to, I was able to realize how important it was to me to experience the sacrament of Matrimony.

I'm skipping ahead a little. I was single a long time, and I moved frequently and lived in different parts of town. As a result, I didn't go to church each Sunday, but at certain times I found a church I loved going to and would go. I met someone at work who was an evangelical Christian. I didn't know what that was, but he introduced me to his church and I attended a few times. A couple from that church met with me. I was annoyed by their approach because they wanted me to believe the Bible in the literal sense. That was not the nice God I had. I didn't believe that if you stole something you literally should cut off your hand. Thus, I was open and I explored some things, but I always found myself back in a Catholic church where I felt like I was home again. I didn't always understand the formality of the Mass, but I was used to it and enjoyed it. I went through periods of going each Sunday but always, I thought it was okay if I didn't. My forgiving God would understand.

Fast forward to once I was married; I still went to church but not as often as I had gone before. Having a non-Catholic husband made it easier for me to miss Mass. Once we moved to Littleton on the west side of Denver and closer to the mountains, I found there were two Catholic churches nearby. I didn't know about them immediately, but most of my friends from the Single Club days (where I ended up meeting my husband) were Catholic. So, some of the good friends I had made in my twenties were Catholic and now many of my new friends I had made in my thirties were also Catholic.

Although Paul didn't practice my faith with me, he was always okay with me doing whatever I needed to do. When Sierra was born, we baptized her in the Catholic Church. When she was a baby I was too stressed out to take her to church with me. Eventually, when she was three or four, I started taking her with me and now I always do. For the most part, she likes coming with me for the mommy time.

In the year when I lost my baby boy and my father, I hit bottom. Depression cloaked me in darkness. I tended not to leave the safety of my home. I knew I needed to be there for Sierra and I was, taking her to preschool and her activities as usual, but my life seemed so black to me then. I went to church which is the only place I felt good. Certain hymns about surrendering to God made me cry each time to the point where I couldn't sing the lyrics even if I loved them. Sometimes Sierra would see my tears, which were a surprise to her. Small things happened to me on the path of being called by Jesus.

First I felt called to commit to a weekly Adoration hour, which I did. Paul could only imagine that I was bored during one whole hour of sitting in the holy presence of the Blessed bread of Jesus. I wasn't sure how it would go, and it wasn't the same every time. I usually would light candles for my father and Matthew, my son. It was comforting to be there with Jesus with the lit candles. In the agony of my pain and my struggle with who I was and what my purpose was, the only thing I could regularly do was go to adoration. There I felt that Jesus had called me to him and I could lean on him. He could understand what I was going through completely. I still didn't always feel at peace, but often I felt it was the only place I could be. I felt closer to each of them and felt like they were close to Jesus. I did plenty of crying, which was the best thing for me to do. There were Kleenex boxes available and usually it was just Jesus and me. Sometimes other people came so I didn't usually cry then, but it was okay too. I found some good books to read while there. One that particularly moved me was a book by Henri Nouwen called *Turn My Mourning into Dancing*. It was beautiful because it didn't say your grief just goes away, and at the time it didn't seem like that would ever happen. The book talked about moving and dancing through it as you move through different stages. That is also where I read the writing of Pope John Paul II, which talked about the meaning of suffering. It is called the Apostolic Letter Salvifici Doloris and it addresses the Christian meaning of suffering. It is a long writing and there was a copy in the adoration chapel. It was good that I was going one hour a week and I could dedicate my time to reading it if I felt moved to, because it takes a long time to read. It was difficult to understand at points and as a person suffering I didn't see why there should be suffering. Nonetheless, certain parts of it were comforting to read at the time. You may find comfort, as I did, reading these three points from the Summary of the original Salvifici Letter at CatholicCrossReference.com. First, the Letter states "Suffering, like all human things, finds its true meaning in Jesus Christ. It is both a burden and a joy. Why it is a burden is evident; why it is a joy requires reflection into the mystery of redemption in Jesus Christ." The second point is "Redemption came through Christ's sacrifice on the Cross: it came through suffering. Thus, our redemption is directly related to Christ's suffering, and our suffering is linked somehow to our redemption." Finally, the Summary concludes that "Suffering is supernatural because God has bound it up with salvation, and human because it is endured by all men. Through human suffering, men find their identity in themselves and in Christ."

Pope John Paul II is the Pope of my lifetime. I have real memories of him as Pope. I saw him in downtown Denver when he was riding in the protected Pope mobile. My friend Julie and I went to see him give Mass at the Vatican while we were there. Even though, mistakenly, we stood in the German speaking Mass line, it was powerful to see him give Mass. Plus, how can you go to Rome and not see the Pope? I didn't know all his accomplishments including this writing, but I was called to read it.

The year Sierra started Kindergarten when she was five, I also started her in the Catechesis of the Good Shepherd religious education program for preschoolers at church. In the process of finding out about this I learned that I could volunteer to teach the preschoolers or be a Catechist. During this period, I met some fantastic people at my church. I found that I was teaching the preschoolers but they were also teaching me. The curriculum covered many of the mysterious aspects of mass that I thought I understood but I didn't. The Montessori based program gives the kids a hands-on way to understand the Mass. My friend Barbara always said the kids were closer to God than we were because their souls were so new. I found that seemed to be true. The kids were encouraged to talk to God either aloud or silently in their hearts. They were encouraged to do this in circle time and during the different learning activities. They participated in prayer. No fighting it, just pure wanting to learn and reach out to God. It was and still is a powerful experience to be with the kids and be in the teacher role.

At this time, I was going to church once a week for adoration, plus going once a week for Catechesis of the Good Shepherd. The next small thing I was called to do was join the Bible Study offered at my church in the format of The Bible In 90 Days Program. I had never really been a Bible person. I knew the two readings in church were from the bible and the Gospel readings were from the Bible, but that was about it for my knowledge. This program was structured for individual participants to read twelve pages a day of the Bible and then once a week we met with a discussion group and watched a video that explained the scripture. It was quite a commitment to keep up with the reading. In particular, it was hard if you got behind by a few days or a week, but I never wanted to go the discussion group unprepared or it felt like it was a waste of time so I kept up. In those moments of reading my twelve pages a day I learned about the Old Testament, which I had never understood. During the readings, I felt like God was talking to me. The stories were about God's love for us and included prophecies for hundreds of years later which one by one came true. I felt like this book, the Bible, told of a powerful plan that spans human existence from the Old Testament to the New Testament; that it was complex and would be difficult to write. I felt called to believe more fully in God and Jesus and I felt God's love. It was good to be with people from church and I was starting to see that my life did indeed have a purpose.

Later, I did a Bible study covering the book Exodus in the Bible. Again, it was a revelation to learn about God's love for us. He wanted a relationship with each one of us. He was patient with the human mistakes we keep making and He kept opening the door for each of us to know Him. I feel completed and supported in a way I haven't before. There is a famous story about a person walking on the beach of life with Jesus and the person asking him, "Why, oh why, in the most painful times in my life did you abandon me?" and seeing where two sets of footprints in the sand became only one set. Jesus answers, "My dear, dear child. When you see times where there is only one set of footprints, it was then that I carried you." That still is very powerful for me. I don't feel like I'm going through life all alone. I might not always understand God's plan for me, but I always believe there is a plan for me that is in my best interest. I feel like God wants a relationship with me and he is inviting me to have one at all moments in my life.

Sierra and I went to a Parish Mission event that was offered some time ago at church and we saw published author and renowned speaker Jim Beckman, who talked about how to journey through Lent. One year for Lent I focused on daily prayer because I understood that my relationship with the Lord is everything.

That relationship helps me, it makes me a more giving person, a stronger person, a more loving person, and it helps me stay open to the will of God for me in my life. The prayer pathway supports me in my search for the meaning of my life and it encourages me when I'm troubled. I still grieve and mourn the loss of my son, the loss of my father, and the loss of my health since MS. However, I don't feel sorry for myself anymore. My biggest agonies through these experiences were due to unrealistic expectations of how my life should go. Now I know that life is hard for all of us in many ways. Jim Beckman spoke about suffering and it closed the loop for me from my reading of Pope John Paul II until now. We all have crosses to bear. They're not all the same, but they all represent trial and suffering. The Christian meaning of suffering is to complete Jesus' suffering. He suffered and died on the cross for our salvation and he did this fully and completely. We are the body of Christ, one community, deeply connected to each other and Christ. As individuals, we all must carry our crosses to complete the suffering of Christ for the total Community. It's difficult to understand, but tragedy is the work of the Evil One, not God. Our relationship with God, which he continually offers us, is the path to healing from our suffering. The path to healing is individual and unique to each of us. If we commit to our relationship with Christ and for our complete healing we then move into a place of service. It is here that we can explore our purpose in this life. We can see that life is difficult for a lot of people, many have it worse than our suffering. When we see that, we see we can help those of us who have fallen on hard times and especially those of us who are worse off. As we grow in our relationship with Christ we see that we must do this. It is our purpose as human beings. Our journeys here on Earth are short compared to our eternity. What are we going to do to make the best of it? What are we going to provide to humanity that humanity must have? How are we going to leave this Earth better than we found it? We need to pray about these questions and ask for the courage to act when we need to act. It is here that we move beyond suffering and into joy and purpose, and it is here we matter. Best of luck to you on your exploration of your purpose. Know that you are not alone. We are connected not just to God but to others. The path of life is wondrous, and we will meet the people with whom we are meant to share our path. The collective consciousness of our role as human beings will solve all the problems of the world and bring us all to a better place. Our children can indeed look forward to a better life than ours when we adults focus on our wondrous life journey and our relationship with a higher power to find our most important unique purpose.

I have had struggles with understanding what my purpose is. I thought it was to have a great career, but then I was disabled and the Universe was specifically telling me to find something else. I thought my purpose was to have two children and a family of four, but then I learned I had Endometriosis and couldn't get pregnant naturally. After navigating the path of infertility treatments which resulted in Sierra's amazing miracle birth and after the loss of my son, I conceded that my purpose was not to have a large family.

During my darkest times of grief, I involved the church in the events I just described and had them pray for the souls of my father and my son. I am so thankful I did. I received a call from someone in the Emmaus Ministry, which is the Grief Support Group. Emmaus refers to the story in the Bible where the disciples were walking on the road to Emmaus and were grieving the death of Jesus. They came upon a man on the road who also was walking. It was Jesus who had been crucified, died, and was buried. He had risen from the dead and now walked and talked with them. Their eyes were blind and they did not see who he was. Jesus walked all the way to the city with them explaining the word of God to them, had supper with them, and disclosed who he was, then disappeared. The disciples asked each other "Were not our hearts burning as Jesus talked with us about the scriptures?" (Luke 24:13-35) I attended support group meetings and met wonderful encouraging and empathetic women. Now almost nine years later, I read the words of scripture with new awareness and find them to be helpful and hopeful to me. I took myself out of life in the years after I lost my child and my father. How much more could I have been living those years had I understood how my pain was a blessing in that I heard the calling of Christ? I now have an acute awareness of the Holy Spirit's power in my life. What this means to me is that I do have a purpose and it is to be a resource to all who have suffered in similar ways as I have. I'm grateful that I could hear this calling from God and to feel the Holy Spirit being present in my life.

Chapter 14

MY AMAZING HUSBAND

Every loving thought is true.
Everything else is an appeal for healing and help,
regardless of the form it takes.
— A Course in Miracles

I've been telling stories about me and my experiences in this book. Doing that gives an incomplete picture because my husband Paul is the thread that weaves through these stories and these are his experiences too, though from a different perspective than mine. Paul has had his disappointments and has had to change his expectations too. I can't tell his story of what it is like to be married to me, but I will share how he's helped our family through all of this.

I sat down with Paul on a date night recently to talk about his perspective. When he found out I had MS three weeks before our wedding, he was surprised and shocked. His perspective has always been and will continue to be that life is complicated. He sought out as much knowledge about MS as he could. In general, he thinks it all works out in the end. In life, you've got to keep moving forward, around and through the obstacles. He was supportive and caring and helped me through the immediate stresses at that time. We moved forward with our marriage and we continued fun activities like we did before we were married. We skied, hiked, camped, biked, traveled, visited both of our families, and enjoyed our lives as a couple. We did all that and we both worked in busy, time consuming jobs. He was my partner and best friend.

Then we both wanted to start a family. He was interested and supportive during the process of figuring out why we weren't getting pregnant. He always knew all the details and facts of each part of the process of diagnosing and treating and what doctor appointments and procedures I was having before and during IVF. He was my support after my surgeries. We had friends who were going through some of the same things, including IVF. He always understood what the doctors were doing and saying at each step. He knew the odds and the risks, and always remained optimistic and accepting when we had to adjust our expectations to a new expectation. I think that is how he helped me the most. I was caught up in the disappointment I was feeling while he was adjusting and seeing all the good happening in our lives.

During the long six-week period Sierra was still in the hospital, we would visit her. I would go during the day with my packed lunch and plan to be there at least long enough to pump in their pumping room each time. The nurses helped me to bathe and feed her. Paul learned everything I learned and even gave her the first bottle when they took her off gavage feedings (this is a method where a very small tube is put through her little nostril and into her tummy directly). He would come and be with her after work to do small tasks we could do to help take care of her. During this time, he was also studying to get his real estate license. I was amazed at all he *was* doing and all he *could* do and manage. Every step the nurses were teaching Paul and me about our new baby. He knew and did everything I could do (except provide the milk). Since Sierra was mainly bottle-fed he could share in the feeding responsibilities too. He was my lifeline and he kept me sane when I was struggling with postpartum depression and adjusting to parenthood. It is an adjustment becoming a family of three not two. After my maternity leave, I returned to work. Paul had always planned to take a leave from work for twelve weeks under the Family Medical Leave Act (FMLA). He took that leave after I returned to work, so Sierra could stay at home with us for 5 1/2 months instead of heading off to daycare six weeks after she came home. We both just had to adjust and change our expected leave times around a February delivery instead of an April one like we had thought.

When Sierra did come home from the hospital she weighed a still small 5 pounds. We put her in her first car seat, which faced backwards, and I was nervous about her being in the back seat while I was in the front seat. The smallest and tightest head supporters on the car seat still left space between them and her little head. So, for the drive home I sat in the back seat with her. As a couple, we were happy to be taking our little girl home at last. Paul in his infinite planning and wisdom was already finished painting and decorating her bedroom and had the last of her new furniture set up the week before she was born. It turned out she didn't need it yet because we had her in a co-sleeper alongside our bed. When she came home she was on a heart monitor that made an alarm signal when her heart rate was higher than normal. She had had bradycardia in the hospital, which meant her heart was speeding up too high. I had wanted her near us in her newborn months anyway and now with her being on a monitor her bedroom across the house seemed too far to me. When her alarm sounded, which it did the first night we were home with her, we were supposed to check her and see that she was still breathing and pick her up if she wasn't. We never had any actual problems but the way the monitor was attached, we had plenty of false alarms when she wiggled in the middle of the night. It was just another worry for us. Of course, like full-term babies, pre-term babies are up in the night frequently.

In the hospital, Sierra had been on a four-hour feeding schedule, which gave us a four-hour block to sleep in the night the two times we stayed overnight with her in a room without nurses. As soon as we were home she was on a three-hour feeding schedule so now there were only three hour blocks available for us to sleep. Paul helped me with the around the clock feedings during the two weeks he took a vacation from work. We had many humorous moments at three a.m. when the diaper changes were messier than expected, and we could laugh together. We learned early on about replacing sheets and clothes more often than anyone could have expected. Again, I was grateful for his help in all areas of taking care of an infant. We had fun doing that together.

It was a different story after his two-week vacation was over and he went back to work and needed his sleep and I took all the feedings at night and during the day. Gradually as the blocks that I slept well got shorter and shorter I had a hard time managing it. I pumped my breast milk because Sierra wasn't breast feeding well; now my blocks of sleep were taken up with taking care of the baby and pumping around the clock. My ability to think and moderate my mood got worse and worse. I got what felt like post-traumatic stress disorder symptoms from all that had happened, because I would jump with a flight or fight response at the sound of Sierra's cry or the sound of her heart monitor. I felt terribly sad about this. Here was the baby I had always wanted and I wasn't able to enjoy all the newborn moments the way I wanted to. Right before I went back to work when she was about twelve weeks old, Sierra started sleeping through the night. I had to go back to work and part of me was happy to have a routine and socialization that was different than staying home all day. Of course, another part of me was experiencing guilt and grief for lack of a full-term pregnancy and for not being able to breast-feed my baby.

Paul stayed home and took care of Sierra after I went back to work. We both got to know the joys and frustrations and sometimes boredom of taking care of an infant. However, Sierra was tiny, and we couldn't imagine anything else and certainly not daycare. Of course, Paul thought staying home was easy because he got a good night's sleep regularly. Because of the way, we arranged our time off, Sierra was around seven months before she was in a daycare environment. We always had her in a home day care not a large facility because we couldn't imagine doing otherwise. Ideally, I would have stayed home full time. We made it work and the blessing was that Sierra grew and thrived no matter what.

Paul anchored my sanity. I tended to stay home, but he is the one that planned the special outings and activities we had with our baby. We took her to downtown Littleton and walked around to look at the shops. We planned a big day taking her up to Estes Park where we had honeymooned. I was uncomfortable and unsure about taking a baby away to different places. He helped me figure out just taking a diaper bag and packing a back pack with her feeding supplies: first it was formula; then it was baby food; then it was baby snacks and baby food. Because Paul almost always creates systems for what he does, I could follow the process when we were together and when I was alone with Sierra. That system helped me tremendously. We then could travel with her. We took many plane trips while she was under two years old and she traveled for free on the airlines. We visited family and traveled to different parts of California several times, as well as San Antonio, Ohio and Michigan. Our routines were gradually becoming more normal like when we were just a couple.

As you've already read, when Sierra was two years old, my cognitive symptoms worsened to the point I got additional testing. Paul supported me while I received the test results and we made the official decision that I would leave work on disability. Once again Paul was going through all of this with me and adjusting his expectation that we would both be working and earning good salaries, to an acceptance that now I would not be working and earning a salary. It was good this process took a few months as it gave us a chance to absorb what my loss of work meant and the appropriate steps I should take to file for short-term disability, then long-term disability. Once I left work for the last time on March 2, 2006 at age thirty-nine, we were in a new reality. At that point, all the family finances were Paul's responsibility and I had no idea what my future looked like for the years ahead.

When I became disabled from my career and ability to work full-time, the blessing was I could now stay home with Sierra. Paul continued at his software consulting job. He had worked as a full-time employee at a National Corporation (the Company) back then partly because they had insurance that covered IVF. That was also where he worked to be able to take FMLA for twelve weeks. Working there was a real sacrifice for him. Big companies can be so inefficient and bureaucratic. So, I know the relief he had when he left the Company eventually and found a new job with a company that hired him as an independent contractor.

Paul is the rock of the family. No matter what happens he can be stable and consistent. Those qualities provide a huge relief and support to me. Sierra feels this too. She always stays aware of Daddy's schedule and checks to see if Daddy is home. If I tell her he has left for the day, she wants to know where he is and when he is coming home. Truly, all is well when Paul is home. He helps me get my bearings, solve problems, and make better decisions. I know this can feel like pressure and a burden for him, but he is Sierra's and my rock.

Paul reminds us to laugh. He has a wonderful sense of humor. I love it when he lets his sense of humor out. He can be so silly and find the joke in everyday things. His delivery is serious and he repeats what he means as a joke repeatedly. Soon, Sierra and I are giggling when we realize he is kidding with us, helping us all be less serious and more fun.

He knows how to see the joy in life even when things are hard. I used this to remind me that there was life out there and outside our home even when we had a preemie newborn or a young baby; even while I was adjusting to the loss of my job as my identity; even when my cognitive problems made things harder on him. It's amazing how much fun we have together.

We liked camping trips and we found ourselves shopping for and purchasing a hard-sided, covered, pop up camp trailer. Paul was an Eagle Scout who had roughed it throughout his lifetime, made major concessions with this purchase. The trailer has one queen sized bed, one full sized bed, a dining room table, shower, toilet, heater and air conditioner, water heater, stove, oven and refrigerator and freezer. We bought the trailer while I was pregnant with Sierra's younger brother. One of the reasons I liked it was that I thought it was perfect for a family of four. My family of six camped in a similar pop-up camp trailer when I was growing up. We used it for one long weekend trip with the four of us, while I was pregnant.

Paul continued to do many things for us while we only helped him a little bit. We spent the summer after my father died taking driving and camping trips across the country and into Canada. It was hard for me to go at first, because I thought of our son Matthew so much. I couldn't lay in my bed in the trailer without thinking that last time I slept there, Matthew was in my tummy and all had felt so right with the world at the time. Paul packed the trailer, I helped with laundry and what food we needed to have packed. Sierra couldn't help much except to stay out of the way. Paul got the set-up of the pop-up down where he could set it up completely by himself in a matter of minutes. We had a great time on our road trip that summer even though there was grief laced throughout our adventures, especially for me. I am so grateful for everything Paul did for us in that period! He really took care of Sierra and me.

After I lost the baby I could see my father one last time where he could speak. Around August 19th he had been admitted to the hospital and couldn't speak because he was on a breathing tube. By September 8th he was gone. Paul completely supported me during this time. After we had got back home, I found a support group of couples grieving the early loss of their pregnancies, their babies. Paul was not crazy about being in a support group and he grieves differently than me, but he continued to walk the journey with me. He was by my side in the group and we made it to every meeting. I love him for that.

Paul continued to work, provide for our family as well as helping in some way on everything. I'm sure this time was hard on him, but he continued to be the rock of the family, bringing humor and fun to our activities anytime he could. His stability and knowing that he stood by me was everything to Sierra and me. There were a lot of hard times for me dealing with knowing Matthew was my last child. I focused on Sierra's preschool. There were times I couldn't have gotten up and lived if I didn't feel my responsibility to her. That is when I would leave the house and sometimes be able to laugh. Paul was readier to adjust to our family as it was. There were difficult times when my longing to be a mother again and his contentment really caused a divide. Gradually I accepted it by focusing on what I do have and not what I don't. Again, he has an amazing ability to handle changes and he was always supporting and helping me.

Eventually, I felt like I woke up and stepped back out into real life. Time healed a lot of wounds even though many events still make me sad. Thankfully, I don't have to live in them anymore. Paul and I had more fun together that year. In October the next year, after our summer of camping, Paul had also started learning and growing through personal development classes that seemed to renew him and make him happy. We camped but not as many trips. Sierra grew and changed and started kindergarten. The following summer, I wanted to find out what all the fuss was about and took my first Millionaire Mind Intensive, as I explained in Chapter 11. It was natural that if he had liked the ideas of entrepreneurship and personal growth then I would as well. I came home with renewed energy, which was exciting for me and I'm sure him. We traveled as a family on a trip to Palm Desert where we took a course together while Grandma and Grandpa watched Sierra.

We have had wonderful personal growth and amazing times as a couple. I started writing this book because I felt so much more creative and confident, which was so fulfilling to me. It's been a long journey, but I feel I'm meant to share what happened to our family and provide our story for others' benefit. I know other people are having at least a glimmer of some of my experiences and I would like to help people not feel as alone as I did. Everyone needs a support system. Paul is part of mine. He's walked the journeys in this book with me. He continues to be a support to me and he is very involved with our daughter Sierra. He lives his life with love and integrity and I learn from him. I am blessed to have such a great man as my spouse and I thank God for it every day.

Everyone needs a support system.

Chapter 15

CREATING A SUPPORT NETWORK

People will forget what you said,
people will forget what you did,
but people will never forget
how you made them feel.
— Maya Angelou

It was a shock to move from perceiving myself as a 'normal' person living a typical life to becoming a person experiencing life on my individual path. What I mean by normal is that I would grow into adulthood, have a career, eventually meet and marry the right man for me and start a family. I would probably have two to three children, and my children would have a happy childhood like I did growing up. As a child in a family of six I leaned towards the three or more children (okay, probably not ever four) since that is what my parents did. Paul on the other hand, was one of two, and in his mind, we would have two children; boys, he hoped, as his parents did. I lived in a bubble of being able to create exactly the kind of life I wanted. As I progressed through college, passed the CPA exam, and found a job working as a CPA at a public account-ing firm (the best of the best possible career path, in my mind at the time), this was a reasonable belief for me.

As you now know, my path diverged from this ideal nor-malcy three weeks before my wedding when I got the diagno-sis of a degenerative disease. That was extremely difficult for me to learn about and to adjust my reality to a new unknown truth and future. No one ever knows their future. That usu-ally does not paralyze most people. For people with a known but still unknown future like people diagnosed with Multiple Sclerosis, it can be difficult. You keep hoping for a great future and try not to let in any negative information, because all that does is scare you. Paul and I didn't plan for our future with MS even though now we knew about it. When we sold my house, and bought our new house, we looked at houses with two levels because that is what we wanted and had imagined for ourselves. Some people might have planned to buy only a one-story in case down the road I couldn't have managed the stairs. We also made a common Generation X error be-cause in our adult lives, housing prices always went up, stock markets always went up, and any debt could be paid off with leverage down the road. For example, my car loan was paid for when I sold my house for a tax-free gain. Now we made a financial error. We took the mortgage I had been paying with my job plus the mortgage Paul was paying with his job and added them together to determine which new house to buy. Neither of us thought about the potential for one of us not to be working. We knew we wanted kids, but we didn't plan for one of us to be a stay-at-home parent. Our group of friends at all these stages were doing the same thing we were doing, and it didn't seem out of line even for our situation.

I had a terrible time adjusting to the fact that I no longer had my health, something I had taken for granted up until then. I didn't talk about it with friends because I felt there was a stigma attached to it. I didn't talk about it with work contacts because there was a real stigma attached to it, since accuracy, attention, and overall brain health was a requirement for the type of work that I was doing and that I had trained to do. So, who did I talk to and how did I handle this BIG SECRET all by myself?

When I first had my vision problems and got my initial diagnosis I had two cats, Fluffy and Cheeto. They were my connections and comfort and they were always reliable and there for me. While I was going from doctor to doctor and to the test that diagnosed me I was experiencing real symptoms. I had trouble seeing my computer screen at work. A good friend of mine had taken me to get my make-up done by a professional specifically for my day as a Bride. They do these consultations for free with the thought that when you see how great you look, you will probably buy the make-up they used. I did exactly that, so I had my look ready for my special wedding day.

My cat Fluffy had enormous beautiful eyes and he was, as the name implies, very, very, very Fluffy and a little bit plump. I often thought that when we had eye contact, he literally could see inside of me and I felt like it was a two-way process or two-way communication. When I was scared and by myself with him I would cry. He could see me, and he knew that I was sad. His open eyes asked me what was wrong. My eyes told him I didn't know yet and explained that I was in the process of figuring it out. In one of these moments, his eyes, or a spiritual message came to me as clearly as if it he had spoken. "Don't worry. You will receive negative news, but it won't be as bad as you are thinking right now. It is not life-threatening. You will be okay." I held that message in my heart, even in the worst of times. My experience was so real and I often thought about it as my diagnosis came from the doctors that this message had been so right. Almost seventeen years have passed since that moment. I received bad news and I do have a degenerative disease with an unpredictable future. Still, I am okay and in many ways, I am living a better life now than I was then.

MS has another symptom that is very common which is depression. Pre-MS I had struggled with depression. I had various periods of my life where I was taking prescription anti-depressant medicine. It is an inherited struggle seen in other family members over time. No one understands the cause of the depression seen in MS patients. All they know is that there is a correlation with depression. The lifetime risk of major depressive disorder (MDD) in persons with MS is estimated to be 50% (Goldman Consensus Group, 2005). No one has documented a single medical reason caused by MS that makes this relatively common. On the face of it, wouldn't it make sense that a life-long degenerative disease would be a depressing scenario if viewed by an outsider objectively? Additionally, the MS disease-modifying therapies almost all had a percentage of clinical trial patients experience an increase in depression while being treated with those specific medications. The interferon medicines, Avonex, Rebif, Betaseron work in a certain way that affects mood. Depression has been one of many struggles I've experienced. Also, I have had periods of time where I struggled to sleep well and often have had insomnia where I wake up in the middle of the night and don't feel as if I will ever fall asleep. So, I take medication which has worked well in helping me reduce this problem.

I need to sleep well and be fresh for my thinking processes and brain to function well, but the lack of sleep, cognitive problems, and depression make up a vicious cycle. Depression can contribute to insomnia, causing lack of sleep, which increases cognitive struggles, which leads to depression which leads to insomnia where you can feel like you start all over again. That cycle makes me never want to stop taking my drugs, even though I sometimes struggle with the side effects. I can go long periods of time with good, regular rest, which helps my cognition and reduces depression bouts.

Not sharing my specific struggles with friends was hard to deal with in my first years of MS. During this time, the biggest Support Network I established for myself was seeing a therapist on a weekly basis. I had a particularly great one and it was so helpful to have an attentive ear to talk to about nothing but my experiences and myself. She was someone who knew my MS history and was there for me when I had my fertility challenges and the births of my two babies. I could share the beginning of a story and she knew all the pieces and how they related to each other. I rarely had to complete all the details because she was already there with me. I relied on this to support me for close to five years. She is a big reason I want to tell my story. I feel so strongly that my experiences will be a support for others who even identify with a fraction of the stories in this book.

One of the support systems I found helpful were MS support groups. I met some great people in these groups and I felt extremely supported no matter what was going on with me. I made some great friends. Many of the people that I've met have wonderful attitudes and dispositions to life regardless of the heartache that has affected them. I feel encouraged and lifted by the demonstration of these characteristics. Often there is a distinct difference in the disease course that we each experience which directs me away from feeling sorry for myself and helps and encourages me to live in a state of gratefulness and grace. I remember how lucky I am and how well things keep working out for me in life, even when terrible things happen. I am not journeying through life alone.

My premature pregnancy loss group provided the same grace for me. Having a safe place to share our experience brought Paul and me closer together. I feel like I was lucky to receive Paul as the perfect husband for me and I shudder when I imagine married life with any of my old boyfriends. None of them are the men that my husband is. He is generous and caring and even when things are hard, he is so reliable and worthy of my trust.

I ended up with the perfect, right sized family for me, especially with the MS reality that I live through daily. Sierra is truly a miracle many times over to me. I learn every day from her even as she learns from me. We are a good team. Our small family unit is perfectly special, and we have such fun times together. When I see women with many kids I can visualize my limitations and what hard work and endurance it can be in some situations. I can enjoy and appreciate Sierra. Even though I lost Matthew, it is a relief not to have stretched my capabilities and be in a position of letting him down. It would have been difficult to be a great mother to both children. I appreciate never having been in the position to abandon or disappoint either child when I have so many daily struggles and it is so hard for me to switch attention between tasks. No mother ever wants to let her children down. Still, none of us are perfect.

For me, a significant support system has been my spiritual faith and relationship with Jesus Christ. Even though I had known and believed in Him my whole life I wasn't the one who sought out spiritual guidance. I believe Jesus called me to serve and to deepen my relationship with him. I just had to keep my mind quiet long enough to hear the call. Spiritual understanding helped me to move forward and truly enjoy my life. Seeing my life from a higher perspective helps me see the divine order in my life. Focusing outside of myself on others helped me to see the world around me more lovingly and over time I didn't feel my deepest pains as much. But I don't have to suffer so much either.

At different times the people who support me change. I meet new people all the time. I never assume that there are chance experiences. I always assume my path crosses the paths of the people I'm supposed to meet when I'm sup-posed to meet them. I usually can feel an emotional con-nection with people to whom I relate. I assume there is a reason when I meet people and I just should stay present to learn what the reason is. I pay attention to what I feel like the Universe is telling me. I trust my gut instinct, when I can feel a reaction in my body that is positive or negative. I'm not always right, but I feel like someone is watching over me always and when something doesn't go my way there is a reason for it and a lesson to be learned. I sense grace and meaning in the slow, sure weaving of my path through life. That is my grand support network and I am never alone!

Chapter 16

EXPECTATIONS AND DISAPPOINTMENTS

He is a wise man who does not grieve
for the things which he has not,
but rejoices for those which he has.
– Epictetus

Peer pressure starts at birth. We don't have the capacity to understand or notice it until we are old enough to be mature. Nevertheless, every child's development is under some microscope. The pediatrician is the first reference point to looking at a child, assessing if it is developing "normally." As a first-time mother, I heavily relied on and looked to the medical professionals to tell me how my baby was doing. The fact that Sierra was born eight weeks prematurely and lived in the NICU her first six weeks of life exaggerated my reliance on the nurses and my unsteady belief in my instincts. Being the worrier that I am didn't help me manage the stress, though I know many other mothers handle things differently compared to me. My point is this: we are measured, assessed, and compared our whole lives. Add a perfectionist tendency and other *oldest child* characteristics and you have a person who constantly compares and assesses who she is in comparison to her peers.

It sounds like I had no confidence or self-esteem as I re-read this. Please remember I considered myself a self-help expert in my twenties. I did have good self-esteem; maybe even to the other extreme. I measured myself ahead of others. Starting when I learned to read and when I was in a higher-level math class, I saw myself as an achiever and someone who would have the life that I wanted. I had some amount of personality tendencies that made it likely that life events like being the first-born child would accelerate the achievement-focused life that I led. But my strategic behavior continued and was created by my actions and my choices. I sought the achievement oriented career of working for a Big 8 (in my day, now the Big 4) public accounting firms. That created a continual cycle of achieving and having to perform at a certain level and in a certain way. The first year in public accounting and every year after I was in a peer group and got evaluated compared to other members of that peer group. I didn't stop to look around and think about what I truly wanted to do with my life until I left that environment at twenty-eight years old. Looking back, I think I forgive myself and can see that I created structure in my life that I felt I needed for some reason. I consciously chose a logical and practical degree like accounting over a writing career. I had some talent in that area, but let's face it, I was the person who had to pay the bills and take care of my life, and I trusted the logic and practicality more than I trusted the creative life, which seemed more unstable to me.

Having a normal life was a basic expectation for me. Normal looked like having a career that supported me financially, friendships, and fun activities; someday I would get married and have kids. I think most of us think this basic framework will bring a happy life. I was shattered and stressed when the last of my good friends got married, when I was 30. It was a horrible feeling for me. I felt lost and uncared for and alone. I was so surprised to notice that a normal girl like me was now an outsider who was different than everybody else my age. I lived my life normally and I would have expected to get married by this point in my life. I can remember the pain of this with clarity. The mere fact of having a girlfriend get engaged triggered all kinds of feelings of abandonment for me.

Was the situation bad or was my expectation and reaction what made it painful? The idea of a good friend getting married would lead to normal feelings from adjusting to having married friends as well as single friends. Was it so bad? It was a happy event for my friend, and I was happy for her. Should I have felt abandoned? Nothing had changed for me. I took care of myself before and I would continue to. The reality was that I hadn't had any focus or intention on being married since I was busy and happy and focused on my work. I could have a responded to the *event* in a way that was kinder and gentler to myself. I was assuming if someone else had a wedding, I was somehow going to be unable to marry. Also, I realize now and I didn't know then that there are many different paths in a healthy life. I thought there was but one path, which created a scarcity mentality; that wasn't accurate.

Looking back now, I know that I met and married the perfect man for me. Any complaining about those times is almost telling the Universe that it was too slow or not supportive of me. Neither of those assumptions is correct nor helpful to keep in my head. Not only was I going to meet and marry the right man, but the timing was exactly as it should have been. Our intellectual brains get in the way of just accepting the way life works. I'm a planner and doer, but I couldn't have planned and done this! The Universe or God can know me and knows how to put the pieces together. When I allow that to sink in, I'm more in awe of God's responsibilities. I realize how difficult it would be for me to multi-task and manage all the pieces the way God does.

What do you do then, when life does not turn out the way you planned; when you had an expectation and the outcome disappointed you? When really bad things like disability or death happen to you? Breathe deeply and find your calm center. Be the ultimate support for yourself. If you need to rest, rest. If you need to act to find a friendly ear to talk to, find it. If you need to reach out to experts who can help you, you should do it. There are support groups for all kinds of things. Meeting other people who know exactly how you feel is a tremendous resource and it is out there for you. Treating yourself like a precious gem will make you strong. I've found online support with groups of women who gave birth because of my exact condition. I have a wonderful group of friends living with MS who I met in a support group that meets once a month. My church has a grief support group which helped me hang on in the middle of my great depression. My doctor connected me with a local group of families who lost children during pregnancy. Finding these resources will support you when you can't support yourself.

The deep pain of loss goes away with time. I used to cringe and hate this advice in the middle of my pain. Grief, however, is a process to be lived through in its own time. One of the next things you need to do is focus on trust. A higher power or the Universe will support you and it has infinite wisdom about timing. By doing daily tasks and routines that make up your life, wisdom and care will come to you. People and other resources like books will find you when you are ready. Focusing on giving thanks for the blessings in your life that are already there is very powerful. I lost my son, but I have an amazing daughter who gives me joy. The daily parental tasks that are part of my routine are easy because they are the most important thing I have on my plate right now. Sierra comes home from school at 3:30. We have homework and sometimes activities to keep us busy. Even when my MS makes me feel tired towards the end of my day, I keep going, because those things are so important and such a blessing.

The old saying about making lemonade when life hands you lemons is true. It is not always easy. Focusing on what I'm happy and grateful about lifts me up. Feeling sorry for myself does not. Even when I'm tempted to go back to feeling sorry for myself because I see someone pregnant with their third child, or I perceive someone to have more energy and a quicker mind than me, I should see that I'm about to go down that path. I acknowledge what is happening inside. If I don't have it in me to join the conversations about babies and pregnancy and growing families, I try to be understanding of myself. Each time this happens and I don't "say should" to myself or beat myself up, I grow stronger. I know over time (it is already happening) things that remind me of my losses will get less painful. Eventually, I won't even see the situation as painful. I give away more and more of Sierra's baby things as time passes and it is not painful to me. I kept many of them because I thought we would have another child. Now it is more powerful to clear out clutter and free up our minds and energy for new wonderful things to come in.

Having goals and dreams is good for people. It gives them what they need to wake-up and energetically live their day. I am happy now because I'm working on this book; it is a good goal for me. What I didn't used to know, but now I do, is when to adapt. Sometimes on the way to a goal we learn that it may not happen the way we planned. Different timing and different outcomes are signals to us. I was sorely disappointed and stopped in my tracks when I got these signals. I wanted to proceed and make my perfect life plan no matter what. As a recovering perfectionist and the first-born in my family, I often set the bar so high for myself unnecessarily. Life can be happy and meaningful without perfection. I only had one place I could go, depression and pain. Have you met people who seem happy all the time? I have, and I tend to be suspicious of them. Don't they have a goal or a problem that is always moving them forward? Enjoying each day and being happy even if you have a problem is remarkable to me. Can it be that life could be as simple as that? I am learning now to enjoy life, each breath and each moment. I enjoyed the joyful moments in my life before. It was difficult, though, for me to enjoy the moments which were not full of the joy I expected—or even worse (surprisingly), the moments which were just mellow. I was so achievement-oriented that my self-esteem would slip when I was able to take it easy. I got bored with the simple tasks of life, like cleaning and laundry. Now, I use the activity as a meditation. I feel love for my family when I'm folding their clothes. I feel good when my house is neat and organized. I can now find joy in these moments. When I was around my father during his illness, I could appreciate how he had lived his daily life. I could see that being up, showered, and shaved was an important accomplishment for him and made him feel good. Those boring, small moments are something to be grateful for. Once he was hospitalized he couldn't do those things anymore. Caring for yourself gives you human dignity, and we take it for granted when we are young and well enough to do it. We forget that all of it is a blessing.

It is painful for me when I realize the many years I was in the doldrums and feeling quite isolated and alone were partly my doing. I forgive myself for each step of my healing. Each step served a purpose for me and was part of a divine plan. I can see now that the speed with which I returned to life and realized how great it was could have been faster. I know that the wizard in me is powerful and I create my life. If I see terrible lonely times that is what I will have. If I see wonder, possibility, and friendship then that will be what I have. That is new knowledge for me. Those people who tended always to be happy were finding things to be happy about. Living in such a way as to expect to be happy is powerful. Yes, there are real disappointments and even tragedies in life. I acknowledge those and know I must undertake a valid grieving process for them. Grief can't be avoided or circumvented. There is life on the other side and you can get there. Lovingly undertake the process, honor the losses you have. However, use your powerful mind to choose to see the wonder and hope that exists in this world. Be humble and grateful and your blessings will be bountiful.

Chapter 17

CONNECTEDNESS

I offer you peace.
I offer you love.
I offer you friendship.
I see your beauty.
I hear your need.
I feel your feelings.
My wisdom flows from the Highest Source.
I salute that Source in you.
Let us work together for unity and love.
— Mohandas (Mahatma) Gandhi

L ife is an individual journey. At least that's what I always thought. Being independent and doing things on my own was a value system I always had. In our egocentric society, it isn't too surprising that this is how I chose to approach life. It took tragedies to shake things up for me. When I had hit rock bottom in any part of my story it wasn't possible for me to operate in the ways I always had. Simultaneous connections started happening to me and I might not have always noticed them at the time, but looking back I can see how things were occurring without effort. As I've related, at the time I was diagnosed with MS, I shared it with my closest friends but was worried about any stigma attached to it in my work life. Since I was so career focused I didn't want people to have a preconceived idea of my abilities or my deficits. But this is no way to live. For the number of hours, I was at work, it was stressful and difficult to never talk to my coworkers about the things I was experiencing and going through.

Therefore, I did some investigating into what MS support groups were out there. There are many around the Denver metro area, but there happened to be one near my home in the suburbs. It met once a month and I reached out to the group. I made some close friendships with women in that group. Probably because 70% of MS patients are women, fewer men attended and therefore I didn't make the same close friendships with men at that time. I remember the first time I met my friend Debbie. She attracted my attention because, like me, she was not disabled in a noticeably physically way. She was young and about ten years ahead of me in her disease course. We connected right away. I didn't see her a lot because we weren't always at the meetings at the same times, but when we were we usually tried to go to lunch afterwards so we could talk more. Gradually, over the course of our friendship we planned outings together every few months or so. When my daughter was in preschool I would bring her with me when Debbie and I were meeting for lunch. She and Debbie developed a separate relationship and friendship, which was fun. Now that Sierra's in school I can't take her as often, but Deb and I continued our opposite side of town friendship. We have certain things in common that have made us grow even closer than when we met. We supported each other in the disability filing process and have leaned on each other when trying to determine our best treatment options. It is great to talk with people who know the language of the life journey with MS. Our friendship continues now but it is truly long distance. She recently moved back home with her family in Connecticut. I'm happy for her and I miss her, but we communicate and stay in touch through Facebook and e-mail.

The fertility clinic we used for our IVF procedures was one of the best in the country. The best doctors and nurses addressed my specific fertility issues there. It was like a little community, because when you are using it and going through the pregnancy process you sometimes spend time there daily and weekly. When we lost our son, the hospital helped me find a support group for couples within fifteen miles or so from us. We could get a babysitter for our daughter so Paul and I could participate once a week. It was helpful again to meet couples who had lost children at various times of their pregnancies. They were quite a bit younger than Paul and me so it was hard because I knew that most of them would move on to having more children, whereas our loss was likely our last pregnancy and baby. Even now though, one thing I've experienced is connections to women at school and/or church who have lost pregnancies early like us. The ones I know ended up having a living child after the loss, but now I can see the context of having a healthy baby as a true gift. God can give life and it is not in my control. I can know, however, that I'm being taken care of all along the way.

I notice now when my path crosses someone else's in a meaningful way. It truly happens all the time. The connections that I'm supposed to have can happen to me when I'm open to it. This happened even more often than the average while Paul and I were taking our personal development courses. Once we were going approximately monthly to our courses we started seeing and getting to know the same people. There were several courses I took alone while Paul was watching Sierra. I found that I regularly sat with the right person for the exercises we would do in certain parts of the course. Usually, I would learn something helpful and meaningful during the discussions I would have with the individual next to me or with a group. I met great friends this way and that I connect with on a regular basis now. It was possible to connect with people all around the world, but I found I made the closest connections with the people we met who live in Colorado. I love staying in touch with this group of people. I treasure my new friendships with these individuals. I know not everyone uses Facebook, but I think it has done wonders for connections between people. I can stay current with friends from many parts of my life very easily. It is nice to find out about people's families and their businesses.

With Facebook, I'm able to connect with my friends from the Mom's Club. I connect with my closest friends I've known close to twenty-five years now. It is wonderful to be able to spend time with people who have known me that long and known me through so many stages of life. I imagine that is just going to get better. I also have friends I met way back when I joined the single's club many years ago now. I don't see them as much as I used to since we are all are busy taking care of our families, and most of us have businesses which keep us busy. I think we are connected to people across the globe, not just our state or even our country anymore. I know women everywhere are dealing with the problems of health and family. We have always carried many responsibilities for our homes and managing relationships. Sometimes this is easier than others, but the statistics on working parents are astounding. According to Ask.com, 75% of families have two working parents. At best, I thought it was always difficult to manage work and home life. It was a challenge when I was single, but I didn't know anything then. Being married to a working husband was easier because there were two people to manage it, but in some ways, it seemed harder: twice as much laundry, for example. Once we had to adjust to a child and there were three of us, it became challenging in a brand-new way. My friends with two or more kids think I don't know anything about things being challenging, because at least I only have one child. None, one or any number after that, life is a challenge for each of us. No one knows when they are born what their crosses will be that they must carry in life, but we all have them.

In church, they say we need to embrace our cross because the other side of suffering is resurrection. It's a concept that can be difficult to understand, but I spent a lot of time thinking and praying about this when I volunteered in the adoration chapel at church. I can see a direct correlation between sufferings in my life and changes in the person that I was, to being a better stronger person now. Would I have been able to experience that if everything was smooth and easy in my life? I'm not sure, but I do believe God has a plan for me and these bumps in the road were ways to get my attention so I could move in a different direction. I'm grateful for every challenge I've had and can see the benefits I've gained. I have a blessed life and over time have come to have more and more joy. I value the connections I've made along my path and I treasure the friendships. I've always found help and support I needed even when I was devastated. Now I know that life has ups and downs for everyone. But all of us are here for a reason and our job is to be open to finding our true purpose. Looking on the bright side and having hope is a way to be that serves us. In my skeptical auditor days, I didn't know that. I was so used to looking for the problem and thinking about what could go wrong. Now I see the infinite possibilities of life and ask questions like, what will go right today? What joy and hope will I find? When I see the world that way, I find the joy and all the possibilities. I notice my daughter's giggling and cheerfulness and I strive to be more like her. She's started humming while she goes about her day, and it surprised me. She didn't learn it from Paul and me! Maybe we should too! She lives in happiness and joy as the normal way to be in life. I want to do that too. I am here to teach her, but I see how she is here to teach me too. And I thank God for her.

I think our biggest connections are spiritual and we don't always see those. That's why I'm sure we are connected globally. Even though we don't know each other we are all human beings and we have the same general concerns and desires in our lives. We need food, water and shelter and companionship and community. We all get scared by anything that interferes with those basic needs. At some level I believe we are all trying to understand our spiritual purpose. I can't understand everything that happens in other parts of the world and in many ways, I take my Caucasian 1st world existence for granted. I might complain about laundry, but I'm not taking it down to the river to do it. I wanted more children, but I'm not living in a place where people need to have lots of children because some of them will surely die or where the mothers often die without medical care. I know I have a lot to be grateful for that doesn't exist for everyone in the state, country, or world.

We truly are all connected to each other and technology and the internet has drawn us a picture of that. We have to work hard to stay ignorant of global life and we live in some of the most interesting times of history. I love that the right people come into my life when I need it. I stay open and I meet people at church that are on similar paths as me. I'm in a Bible study and now I'm hearing about books on spirituality and ways to help me continue to grow. The right people show up for me at the right time. It is a mysterious process that doesn't involve me in making it happen. It is through my connectedness with the people around me that I'm taken care of in the right way and at the right time.

Chapter 18

PERFECT TAPESTRY

In the end, my life has turned out blessed.
Trust me, though, I couldn't have written it!
— Debie Monax

Certain music that I heard when I was young made a real impression on me. The sound of the music connects me to the emotions I had at the time. Carole King's *Tapestry* is a meaningful album for me. I don't know what age I was, but my Mom had bought the album and played it on our record player. I was interested in the player and learned how to pick the album I wanted and play it. Our '70s-style living room had a corner with wood panels alternating with mirrors. There was also a chandelier that hung on a chain from a hook in the ceiling. It was the perfect stage for a girl between seven and eight-years-old to play dress-up and sing from. I would adjust the dimmer switch on the light accordingly and play Carole King's songs, hold a pretend microphone, and sing from the bottom of my heart into the mirror. I knew almost all the words! I missed and remembered the music so much when I was an adult. I looked for it in a music store one time and was so excited one day to find the Tapestry album on cassette tape! My car stereo played cassette tapes so I bought it. My car became my stage, recreated from my youth, and I happily belted out the songs while I was driving to and from work. I still play them in my car on CD every so often and Sierra loves the music too.

Although I knew most of the words on the tracks, one song that stumped me was the title track from the album. I would think about this song, Tapestry, and wonder what it meant. Now, looking back on my life, I wouldn't say I perfectly understand the meaning of my entire journey. But when I think of my life as a tapestry, I can start to make some sense of it. I was so focused on myself and my career when I was young, and in hindsight, I have an understanding of it. I had been in enough situations by then that I needed something, yet had found myself alone. It could be that I needed something from my parents when their marriage was disintegrating; it could be I needed relationships with life-long friends that I never had because we kept moving. I used to be the kid in school that knew everyone, but never had best friends, because I was the new kid. All my close friendships became losses that I grieved.

Finding my footing in a certain career like accounting was comforting to me. There was always a right answer without too many gray areas. I didn't grow up with a set plan to have children. I used to say someday I would–after I had established my career, maybe when I was twenty-five because I thought that was old. I practiced my Catholic faith most of my life, but I didn't have a goal to marry in the Catholic Faith and have a handful of kids. I think you get what you pay attention to. I achieved success at work, but I didn't meet my husband and marry until I was thirty-two. I reflect on it now, and I believe as the path unfolded I always was getting what I needed. Paul and I are perfect for each other and I am glad we are on this life journey together.

I was shocked by my MS diagnosis, and it shook me to the point that I started to examine my life closely. When 9/11 happened a year afterward, I saw how people were in shock and suddenly knew their lives could end and I would say that I already knew that because of my MS. I ended up in jobs where I could be successful without having to work overtime. If I was in a job that wasn't working for me, I was always led to my next one through people that I knew. I never started a job after my first one that I didn't get my interviews through my connections and my network. I left one job without having another lined up, with the intention of writing. My husband was very supportive about it and was fine without my income. In fact, I couldn't handle the lack of structure working from home. When I received a call from a headhunter after four and a half months, I was open to going through the interview process. The new job aligned with my experience and expertise so it truly seemed as if it had fallen out of the sky and into my lap. The economy wasn't great, yet I got this amazing job. I was immensely grateful for this and became even more grateful.

The health care system in our country has been screwed up for a long time, but I couldn't have timed or planned this better for myself. I had been not working and was without insurance at that time. The job that fell into my lap meant I was safely insured. Not being covered would have made MS a pre-existing condition and I would not have been insurable. When I had my first MS symptom and subsequent diagnosis, I was fully covered and even had a short-term disability policy through work. I never thought about that or ever needing it, but when I finally was unable to work and had to leave work, that policy paid half of my income the entire time. Later I qualified for Social Security disability and received that income plus a small amount of short-term disability, which didn't make up for my lost income but was a generous amount for meeting my financial needs. I was not at all aware how to prepare for the unexpected in that way. All the years I'd spent worrying and believing I was in complete control of my life proved fruitless, because I ended up in a place where I had what I needed even though I hadn't even come close to having the knowledge to be able to *plan* it.

I didn't have any worries at all about whether I would be able to have children when Paul and I married. Later, when I learned that there was a high chance I wouldn't have them, the journey towards my pregnancy with Sierra and later Matthew was filled with God's grace even though it was clearly out of my individual or collective control. When Sierra was born early I didn't have any thoughts about premature birth. I had a well-baby check-up and a clean bill of health four days before I delivered Sierra eight weeks early. I checked out Swedish Medical Center as a possible place to go for Sierra's delivery. I never considered Littleton hospital. The day I went to Swedish in pain and learned I would be delivering Sierra that day, I discovered how completely out of control of the situation I was. Thank the Lord that He was in control. I had relatives all over the country in prayer for us after we told our parents the situation. It was a powerful miracle which brought Sierra into this world and allowed me to gaze at her beautiful face while holding her in my arms for a few brief moments before they whisked her away to the NICU. After she was born I learned that Swedish could take care of my baby with a Level 4 NICU while Littleton Hospital was not. We were so lucky to be in Denver where I could have my early delivery and be in the same hospital with my baby instead of the baby having to go out of state to a different hospital. It was not a great feeling to leave the hospital after delivering Sierra without her, but I was lucky because I was only eleven miles from my house so I could go back and forth easily to see her.

I was excited when I found out about being pregnant for the second time. Losing that baby, my son Matthew, was extremely painful. The grace filled experience of delivering him with Paul at my side was a powerful blessing in disguise. I felt God's presence so strongly in the room with us. Now I believe Matthew, though not my ideal way of receiving a blessing, was a blessing nonetheless. I believe Matthew could be in Jesus' arms and be loved without living life on earth which, from everything I hear about Heaven, is the hardest thing any of us will ever have to do. Sierra knows about her brother, and I believe that from Heaven, Matthew can give her strength powerfully. She loves that she has a brother in Heaven even though she misses not having one here.

I was just on a scrapbooking weekend with friends. Paul has always had the belief that we have the perfect, right-sized family for us even when I have struggled with having that belief. When I look at the photos of my family that I scrapbooked I feel such powerful love for them, and I know I am incredibly blessed. The painful events in my life journey don't make much sense when looked at in isolation. But when I look at all of them together there is such balance and grace in all of it. I couldn't have written it, I always say. My life has been designed perfectly to this point. I don't know what the future holds, but I know that it will be the perfect outcome for me. I'm not in control of my life, but my life has a perfect design. It is a powerful and caring love that my God gives to me so mercifully.

I am meant to share my story with all the people in the world who are hurting. Loss engulfs us all at some point. No one should feel isolated and alone in those moments. We need to see those people around us clearly and compassionately. Sometimes a heartfelt hug or a warm hand to hold is all someone needs to pull them back into living life. Lend an ear. Ask the person if they would like to talk to you. Then listen and be with the person. Loss doesn't have to take you away from your life. I believe it will help us live our lives more fully and completely. What is your purpose? How will you leave your mark when you've left this earth? How will people remember you? Take a journey of discovery and see what your path is. This journey is the ultimate in a life well-lived and of leaving this earth better than when you found it. Start your journey today!

Chapter 19

COMING BACK TO LIFE

There are only two ways to live your life.
One is as though nothing is a miracle.
The other is as though everything is a miracle.
— Albert Einstein

In 2008, the Horrible Year, I lost my second baby in my womb and two months later, my father died a painful death from malignant melanoma. I coped with those losses by living for my daughter. She needed me and though I felt like there was no purpose in my life, I made a choice to have her be my purpose. In 2009, we took two long driving trips with our pop-up trailer. I was super depressed at that time and I stayed sedentary. I enjoyed our trip and the relaxation, but I gained weight little by little.

We traveled to Glacier National Park and Yellowstone National Park. Both are beautiful and we did so many activities I soon began to be caught up in them. I focused on the beauty all around me and the moment of time we were in and not just myself. That was the start of coming back to life. My daughter started kindergarten, and we lived happily. In 2009, my husband took a Millionaire Mind Intensive class and began traveling to various courses. In 2010, I traveled to my first Millionaire Mind Intensive by myself. It sparked my interest and I started to see the world outside of loss and disability. I remember being able to get out of bed more easily and even to be happy with my daily life. I give credit to my family for being so supportive and to Paul for finding the path by which our lives would change in the personal development courses he found. In August, we went to a course in Palm Springs and in the fall, we signed up to take all the courses. Later we realized we only had 2011, one year, to take the courses, which we then did. We had to travel for them and coordinate care for our then seven-year-old daughter. It was no small feat to get our plan in place to do this. Few people understood why we would do it, and some people criticized us for leaving our child behind in someone else's care. But I credit the courses for a huge part of coming back to life. I could finally see some purposes for my life and move past survival to thrive. I met great people, learned tons of new things, got lots of ideas, and those things finally moved me away from the disability loss and family losses that had engulfed me. I started writing this book. I could see myself as having something to offer to the world, which was huge. Things that got me moving forward were interaction with what I call the "outside world." I had created a comforting cocoon and a life indoors to help my healing process. I had walked around carrying my grief as a badge of honor. I started to put the badge aside and could speak to moms at Sierra's school who had more than one child. When you have fertility issues or when you lose a child it seems like all you can see around you are pregnant women and women with multiple children. It is hard to sit in church and listen to the talk about stopping abortions. Not that I would have an abortion but I've been pro-choice for years. This past Sunday the same topic came up and I could listen and hear it. I've always had a hard time with that because they are talking about people who voluntarily ended their pregnancies. In my case, I had a perfectly healthy baby inside of me which it felt like God took away from me. How to reconcile that? Since I believe God is the only one who can give life or take a life it is hard not to be mad at God once loved ones die.

After so many months of being sedentary I put on a lot of weight. The weight was bad, but what was worse was the loss of strength I felt. I had lost muscle so I was weak. Worse, I experienced a loss of power. I didn't feel capable or confident. Whenever you have a significant loss such as that of a parent or a child, every other historical loss comes back as if it was fresh. I had real pain and loss, but I felt my other losses as if they had just happened. The grief of my MS diagnosis was there, and the grief over my loss of career and my disability returned as if it had just happened. Even losses that I had felt related to fertility were all rolled up in the loss of my baby. That was overwhelming. No one can stand this for an extended length of time. I knew I needed to exercise for my body. But I also needed to do it for my power. I saw an infomercial about a workout program called P90X. It included DVDs to watch at home and have a gym-like workout without leaving the house. The program was designed to be 90 days long. I was committed to the program and got up early to finish my work out before Sierra woke up. If I got behind because I missed a workout I simply added it back to the end of my four-week commitment or whatever place I was in my workout process. Because of this, my program lasted longer than three months, it was around five to six months. Well, that ended up burning me out so that I didn't keep doing it once it was over. So, what I did next time was keep on schedule with the ninety-day program even if I wasn't perfect at it. Then I could take a few weeks off and start fresh again at the beginning of the program because it was good to make it part of your routine and commitment to staying strong and healthy. I had tremendous results. I lost weight, which was great. Even better, I lost inches in ways I never had before. Also, what I least expected was how much more powerful I felt. My body was physically stronger and I sat up and stood up straighter. I moved with grace and ease throughout my day. My mood improved naturally. Physical exercise boosts our serotonin hormone, which makes us feel better. In the MS research field, they have learned that exercise raises your growth hormone, which is beneficial to the ongoing healing process that occurs in your brain with MS. So, my workout regimen was a key part of digging myself out of the depression hole and changing my view of the world from black and white to being able to see the world in vivid and bright colors again. Being hopeful instead of fearful. Living small instead of living large. I moved from scarcity to abundance. Instead of thinking that there wasn't enough for me, I started to see how abundant and wonderful my life is. I saw unlimited possibilities. Ideas started moving through me and I experienced the feeling with wonder and appreciation. I became less focused on myself and my problems and started to see other people in the world and to focus on them. Being able to do that was amazing and life-changing for me. When you focus on others you can see that the world is not as perfect and sanitary as my expectations about the world had been for me. You see that people have problems and loss of their own. Focusing on how I could help them was empowering. And I really could help them from having experienced the life I had. It finally seemed like my life had purpose and meaning that was all part of the bigger picture. When I stepped outside of myself and saw the world from a new perspective it did seem like my life was taking on a design and I was being taken care of. It was from this place that I could focus on what I was grateful for. I could see and appreciate all my blessings. I could love my family and friends right now. A burden was lifted not having to try to have the perfection that I had previously strived for. I could see and enjoy other people's gifts. My daughter comes in my closet and picks out clothes for me. She has definite ideas about colors and accessories. It is wondrous to see that this is how she views life. She was born that way, I didn't create that in her. Many things take care of themselves.

The activities that I've described above led me out of the darkness of feeling sorry for myself. They flipped the spotlight away from what I didn't have or no longer had onto all the things I did have. My daughter, my family of three, my husband, my home, my great life. I can walk, I can think, and I have talents. I'm not forced to live the "9 to 5" torture most people have if they don't love what they're doing. The more I could change the lenses to see the positive things happening, the more I began to love my life and feel joy with everything in it. Most of us could choose to be grateful for our lives. We are in our youth usually, but as we get older or when things just don't happen like we thought they would it can be hard not to shut down. What I've learned is that I've been given my life for a purpose and shutting down is not an option. It would waste the gifts that I have. I have been through a lot and I have a lot to share with people. It is my duty and my pleasure to do that. When things don't go your way, it is a gift. You can learn and find out what kind of person you are. When you do that you have more to offer the world than you might ever have thought you had. Enjoy the beauties of your world and how amazing your life is.

RESOURCES

These are ideas for places to look for support. All of them have helped me along my journey.

National Multiple Sclerosis Society
    - Find the chapter nearest you for best support.
    http://www.nationalmssociety.org

Rocky Mountain MS Center - Google to find equivalent group
    near you. This was near me:
    http://www.mscenter.org

North American Research Committee on Multiple Sclerosis –
    NARCOMS
    NARCOMS is a research program that allows people with
    Multiple Sclerosis to expedite Multiple Sclerosis research by
    volunteering information about their experience with Multiple
    Sclerosis.
    http://www.narcoms.org

Colorado Center for Reproduction - National Fertility Center
    http://www.colocrm.com

Premature Birth
    http://www.marchofdimes.com/baby/premature_indepth.html

Healing Hearts Baby Loss Comfort
    http://www.babylosscomfort.com/grief-resources/
    https://www.facebook.com/
    HealingHeartsBabyLossComfort

WebMD Grief and Grieving
http://www.webmd.com/balance/tc/
grief-and-grieving-topic-overview

Salvifici Deloris – Letter of Pope John Paul II on the Christian
Meaning of Human Suffering
http://www.catholiccrossreference.com/blog/2014/10/09/sum-
mary-of-salvifici-doloris-on-the-christian-meaning-of-human-
suffering/

Online HELLP Syndrome Group (membership required
http://health.groups.yahoo.com/group/hellpsyndrome/

Groups are helpful and you should search for a group for
you in your area. I also used a personal counselor for some of my
grieving, which was helpful.

American Psychological Association (APA): multiple sclerosis.
(n.d.). *The American Heritage® Science Dictionary.*
Dictionary.com
http://www.dictionary.com/browse/multiple-sclerosis

ACKNOWLEDGMENTS

Thanks to my husband Paul, who patiently waited for me to find my voice and helped me all along the way. Thank you for believing in me!

Thanks to my daughter Sierra who taught me to find love and laughter and who keeps me laughing. You are such a creative and loving human being.

Thanks to my MS doctors who have cared for me since my diagnosis and supported me: Dr. Ronald Murray, Dr. Allen Bowling, and Dr. Beverly Gilder. I so appreciate your care for me.

Thanks to Dr. Eric Surrey at CCRM. Thanks for your logic, caring, and wisdom which helped Paul and me to have our family.

Thanks to the people of Light of the World Catholic church who were there to help support and hold me while I mourned, my faith developed, and Jesus called me. I especially appreciate Father Michael Pavlakovich, Pastor and Reverend Joseph Lajoie with whom I consulted for guidance over the years.

Thanks to my sister, Denise who was always there for me to talk to and to bounce ideas off of on this journey.

Thanks to my mother who helped me proof the manuscript and supported me all along the way in my desire to share my story with the world.

Thanks to the Lord who came through me to help with the words and concepts in my book.

Thanks to my editor, Vicki Tosher who asked all the right questions, which allowed the book to develop.

Thanks to Polly Letofsky who believed I could take this journey before I did.

About the Author

Debie Monax graduated from the University of Colorado in 1990 with a B.S. in Accounting and worked as a CPA for sixteen years, before being diagnosed with MS in 2000. Now, Debie is an author and stay at home Mom. She spends time with her family camping, hiking, enjoying nature, and loves to travel and to cook. In her spare time, Debie is a member of the Better Investing stock club, Women's Investment Team. She currently lives in Littleton, Colorado with her husband, daughter Sierra, and silky terrier Watson. Debie speaks to groups about her faith journey and enjoys presenting to book clubs. To invite Debie to speak at your event, please contact her at Debie@DebieMonax.com.